THE SECRET OF
Writing
Options

LOUISE BEDFORD

Wrightbooks

Also by Louise Bedford

The Secret of Candlestick Charting
Trading Secrets

First published 1999 by Wrightbooks
an imprint of John Wiley & Sons Australia, Ltd
33 Park Road, Milton, Qld 4064

Offices also in Sydney and Melbourne

Typeset in 11.0/12.5 pt Capelli-plain

Reprinted November 2000 and April 2002.

© Louise Bedford 1999

This book is copyright. Apart from any fair dealing for the purpose of private study, research, criticism or review as permitted under the Copyright Act, no part of this publication may be reproduced, stored in a retrieval system, or transmitted in any form or by any means, electronic, mechanical, photocopying, recording or otherwise without prior written permission. Inquiries to be made to Wrightbooks.

National Library of Australia Cataloguing-in-Publication Data:

Bedford, Louise
The Secret of Writing Options: an Australian
Guide to Trading Options for Profit.

Includes index
ISBN: 1 876627 14 X
1. Options (Finance) – Australia.
I. Title.

332.6450994

Cover design by Rob Cowpe
Printed in Australia by McPherson's Printing Group
ISBN: 1 876627 14 X

10 9 8 7 6 5 4 3

Disclaimer
The material in this publication is of the nature of general comment only, and neither purports nor intends to be advice. Readers should not act on the basis of any matter in this publication without considering (and if appropriate, taking) professional advice with due regard to their own particular circumstances. The author and publisher expressly disclaim all and any liability to any person, whether a purchaser of this publication or not, in respect of anything and of the consequences of anything done or omitted to be done by any such person in reliance, whether whole or partial, upon the whole or any part of the contents of this publication.

WHAT PEOPLE SAY.......

This is, by far, the most informative book on option trading I have ever read... By focusing on the practical rather than the theoretical, Louise sets out a clearly marked path which, if followed in the way she suggests, has every chance of producing financial success.

Dr Harry E. Stanton, Private Trader and author of *Let the Trade Wins Flow*

This book is a remarkable introduction to trading in options. It summarises all the experience Louise has gained from her own successful trading ability and from the format of her investment courses. Highly recommended for beginners.

Jim Kirkhope, Private Trader

Louise has managed to take the world of options and make it hers. The simplicity and clarity of her system will complement the strategies available to traders at all levels.

Paul Ash, Victorian President of the Australian Technical Analysts Association

As a private trader, I had occasionally traded in options with mixed results, but had never considered writing them. I had read some theoretical works on option trading, but needed a better grasp of the nuts and bolts. Louise has drawn on her own experience as a private trader to provide a practical, down to earth, and easy to read text which explained to me how to earn extra income while controlling risk. This book is a must read for anyone wanting to cut through the mysteries of writing options and get on with the task of actually doing it.

Jim Edwards, Private Trader

I am an active equities trader who has occasionally covered physical positions by buying options. I wasn't aware that I could also write options until I met Louise. Option writing has provided me with the monthly income that is difficult to achieve in equities trading.

Anthony Torzillo, Private Trader

Louise is a disciplined, consistent trader who has a coherent methodology towards trading the market. She is passionate about what she is doing. Readers will benefit from strategies outlined in this book.

Bill Wee, Director Charting Australia, Supplier of SuperCharts

CONTENTS

FOREWORD

Options writing is typically poorly understood, and more often than not, poorly communicated. This is why it is often dismissed as too complicated or too difficult. So many traders are put off trading in options because they are not very good at it!

Like any skill, writing options has to be learned and practised before it becomes easier and more profitable. If you are keen to acquire this skill it is best to start at the beginning.

Fortunately, if you have come this far and picked up this book then you have realised that you need to know more about options trading. Louise Bedford has been teaching others about options writing for many years and is a successful options trader herself. This expertise shows through in her book in the way she helps novice option traders negotiate the maze that is options writing.

Louise demonstrates that there is far more to trading than understanding the mechanics of how markets work. It involves a method of engaging the market, an understanding of money and risk management and most importantly of all it requires an understanding of the psychological aspects of trading. Only good traders understand these areas and can communicate their importance to others.

The Secret of Writing Options provides a practical and informative introduction for the newcomer to the options market and will give new insights into this area of derivatives trading to the more experienced.

CHRISTOPHER TATE
Author and Trader
Melbourne
October 1999
www.artoftrading.com.au

FROM CORNER OFFICE TO HOME OFFICE...

After a few years of working my way up the corporate ladder, I had managed to carve out a professional niche for myself. As a National Manager for a large multinational company, my professional ambitions had finally begun to come true. Then the unexpected happened.

Over the course of a few short months, I progressively lost the use of my arms through an unexplained tendon condition. I found that even simple tasks such as opening doors had become a day-to-day painful struggle. My responsibilities at work began to suffer as I jumped on the health professional merry go round. From specialist to specialist I travelled. I was informed that it would take me several years to recover. Some of the less positive members of the medical profession did their best to obliterate any hope that I had of reaching a full recovery. I was told that 'You have to be realistic!'

Dressing, driving and feeding myself had now become daily challenges. At this time, I decided to leave my beloved corporate role. Life was looking bleak indeed.

My husband and I had been share trading for a few years and my broker had kept up to date with my situation. He suggested that I try trading options in addition to shares, as a way to produce a regular income. Initially I was daunted by the prospect. After investigating, I was amazed at how simple it was to receive a monthly income based on this innovative way of trading.

Having experienced a health setback, I found that trading provided a welcome diversion to the continual physiotherapist visits. Instead of being stuck at home and bored, trading options allowed me to gain control over a major aspect of my life and provided a reason for getting out of bed in the morning — a much more welcome prospect than becoming a 'couch potato'.

It occurred to me that there must be many other people who have found themselves in a situation where they would like to create a regular part-time or full-time income from their own home. Maybe they have fallen victim to company down-sizing or are finding that they would just like to scale back their hours working for someone else's goals and dreams. Others would just like to give themselves a well-deserved pay rise and develop some control over their own salary package. Some people would even like to work from home so that they can become full-time parents. If this describes your situation, trading options may well be an activity that would be profitable for you to consider.

Over the past couple of years I have had great improvement in the condition of my arms. Today I am a full-time, active, private trader and I am thankful that trading has eliminated the need for me to re-enter the corporate world. By seeing actual trading examples throughout this book you can benefit from the experience that I have gained trading and develop a valuable set of skills that will allow you to make money no matter what the market conditions.

Whilst many traders implement basic options strategies, there are others who have a fascination with complex option trades such as 'condors' and 'butterflies'. Particularly when learning about options, it is best to focus on simple strategies as these complex manoeuvres are out of the comfort zone of many traders.

If your goal is to learn the formalities of the market, and to drown in pages of technical detail, you may as well stop reading now. However, if you would like to learn a simple, profitable approach that is easy to understand and implement, then this is the book for you. My goal is to help you to minimise your losses and maximise your gains using this method of trading. Preservation of capital is of paramount importance, and by learning from my mistakes as well as my wins, you can quickly develop skill in writing options.

Reading this book and working through the examples will assist in developing your confidence in trading options. You will have the chance to experience success with paper trades prior to committing your actual capital to the market. Developing success habits will assist you in trading options profitably.

Trading options represents an effective way to supplement your income, or as your skills improve, to possibly become your main source of income. As your understanding and experience grows, so will your confidence.

I cannot promise that you will make money by simply reading this book. The essence of trading is using the information provided and dealing with

I cannot promise that you will make money by simply reading this book. The essence of trading is using the information provided and dealing with the psychological principles inherent in creating this form of income. Trading excellence will take time and practice to develop. This book will provide you with the necessary tools to succeed, but your application of the techniques will determine your level of success.

LOUISE BEDFORD
Melbourne, October 1999
www.tradingsecrets.com.au

DISCLAIMER

Writing options entails contingent liability if the trade goes against your initial view. You must consult your financial adviser before acting on any of the material contained in this book. Past performance is no guarantee of future profits. The decision to trade, and the method of trading or investing is a personal decision and involves an inherent level of risk.

Chapter One

BOOM OR BUST

The glamour and excitement of the sharemarket! 'Buy BHP, Sell ANZ' cries the trader frantically into his mobile phone to his broker. The smell of fear, the rush of greed... surely these are emotions which inspire traders large and small.

The common perception of successful traders in the sharemarket is that they have high levels of adrenaline combined with nerves of steel. Reality, however, paints a different picture. Often the 'cowboys' of the sharemarket are *not* the traders who are actually making money. In fact, 80% of traders do not make significant amounts of money through trading, and many become so gun-shy that they are unlikely to trade effectively in the future.

However, there is a small but skilled set of traders who consistently take profits from the market and often are quite humble about their accomplishments. Consistent returns of between 20% to 50% each year are common among this group, and they set about their money-making activities with a calmness and clarity which makes a mockery of the emotional trading habits of the sharemarket novice. You probably will not recognise these traders, as often they do not attend many of the mass functions held on 'How to Make Money'. With a cool head, these astute traders identify opportunities and place their orders, taking their wins as well as their losses in their stride. Consistent sharemarket winners have a series of strategies for rising markets, but they also know how to benefit from a sideways or downtrending share.

To which group would you rather belong? What are your reasons for getting involved in the sharemarket? Only you can answer these questions. Are you keen on developing a system of trading that can suit your lifestyle and will allow you to profit from the sharemarket with each passing year, regardless of market conditions? If this is the case, you may find that you will need to add to your current, familiar strategies. Rather than just buying shares and looking to achieve capital growth, it may pay to investigate the derivatives market.

"Consistent sharemarket winners have a series of strategies for rising markets, but they also know how to benefit from a sideways or downtrending share."

Derivatives provide exposure to shares, but they deliver greater leverage. A derivative is a financial instrument which has another asset as its underlying base and includes futures, warrants and options. Rather than purchasing the share (also known as the underlying security), you can trade using a tool that will allow you to make money whatever direction the market is trending. Sounds too good to be true? Perhaps this is only the realm of the professional trader or the domain of the institutional trader?

Actually, it is a field that is growing in popularity by allowing even small investors to benefit from a variety of market conditions. Developing skill in this market will ensure your longevity as a trader and increase your bank balance in direct proportion to your ability to detect trends.

While some traders are getting rich, other traders are consistently making a loss. This is largely due to the strategies that are utilised by winners in the market, and the limited array of methods used by those making a loss. In choppy markets it is essential that you add appropriate strategies to your arsenal in order to consistently make money.

Would you like to increase your trading versatility, make money whatever the economic conditions, and consistently take profits from the market? This is usually the ultimate goal of most investors. If this is your goal, then you will find that trading in the options market will provide all of this and more!

You can learn the secret of writing options which can allow you to consistently make profits regardless of market conditions. Few traders realise that the key to increasing their return on investment lies in this simple strategy. By writing options and learning how to write them well, you have more chance of becoming one of the 15% to 20% of successful options traders who make money in this market.

WHY DO PEOPLE TRADE OPTIONS?

Let's have a look at the main reasons why people trade options. Firstly, option trading is a leveraged tool. It can provide excellent returns from a minimal capital outlay. Leverage, however, operates as a double-edged sword. When you win, you can win tremendously well. When you lose, the leveraged aspect of options can definitely work against you.

Secondly, regardless of the direction of the market, you can make money using different option strategies! Whether your view is bullish, bearish or even if you believe that a share is trading in a sideways band, options can make you money. If you can accurately analyse the direction of the share or index, there is an option strategy that you can use to make a profit.

The other major reason for getting involved in this method of trading is the income-producing qualities that options represent. When trading shares, you do not have the opportunity to benefit when a share is trading in a flat band for example, or going down in value, (unless you short sell the market which is another whole topic). Instead of the 'hold and hope' view that a lot of share investors employ to achieve capital growth, option strategies allow you to frequently take consistent profits from the market. Instead of holding onto shares for months or years, options provide a greater level of flexibility.

Lastly, options traders do not need to analyse a great number of shares. They can focus on only a limited number of liquid shares and their related options.

WHY OPTIONS INSTEAD OF WARRANTS?

A warrant is essentially a long-dated option. The ability to implement a strategy using a leveraged tool is extremely appealing in both the warrant and the option markets, so you need to look at the unique properties of each. If you decide to purchase a warrant, you require the underlying share to trend strongly in order to make money. By purchasing a call warrant you require the share to trend upwards strongly if you are to make significant returns. If you purchase a put warrant, you require the share to trend downwards strongly in order to make a good return on your investment. There are many other types of warrants, but in general, this is the philosophy behind warrant trading.

In the warrant market, if the share trends sideways in a lateral band, you will lose money. This is due to the effects of time decay. Warrants depreciate in value over time. Because of this, you are reliant only on the movement of the share in order to make money on the warrant. The movement of the share must be greater than the effects of time decay, otherwise the warrant will be worth considerably less than when you made your initial purchase.

The situation is the same when buying options. You require the underlying share to trend strongly in the desired direction or the effects of time decay will erode the value of your options.

The major difference that I have found between warrants and options is that the options market represents a greater level of flexibility. Large corporations such as Macquarie Bank issue warrants. Individuals do not have the power to issue a warrant, they can only purchase them.

The options market gives you two choices. You can purchase an option or you can implement an option writing strategy. As an individual trader, you can 'issue' the option and the other party can purchase the option, paying you a 'premium' for the privilege. The option buyer pays you money directly into your bank account, even if you do not own any shares whatsoever. This strategy has the effect of allowing individual investors to have the power of a major corporation such as Macquarie Bank!

Why is it an advantage to have the power of an issuer? By utilising an option writing strategy, you are putting yourself in the enviable position of having sold a depreciating asset. For example, imagine that you own a car dealership. As soon as the first new car drives out of the yard, you would probably be pretty happy with yourself. You have managed to sell the owner of the new car a depreciating asset that loses value as soon as it has travelled a few kilometres. Even if the owner returns the car a few days later and tries to sell it through the dealership as a used car, it would be worth much less than the original purchase price. As the owner of the car dealership, time is on your side as soon as the purchase has been finalised. Option writers find that time is similarly on their side.

When you have sold another trader an option, you have sold him a depreciating asset. Time is on your side. Once the option has been purchased, if it is out-of-the-money at expiry, it will be worthless. You will have the money in your bank account and the buyer of the option will be holding a worthless asset. Although it seems confusing initially, it is possible to sell an option without having purchased an option in the first place. By selling an option to open a transaction, you are granting or writing an option.

More investors lose money when buying options. This contrasts strongly with traders who implement an option writing strategy. In fact, some brokers estimate that up to 85% of people lose money when buying options! It seems that professional traders take the time and the trouble to investigate option writing as a strategy, instead of plunging into option buying as the majority of people do. The subjects that are tricky to learn seem always to earn the most money! Why not put yourself in the position of behaving as a professional trader. Stack the odds in your favour and educate yourself in the field of writing option contracts.

For these reasons, I will be concentrating mainly on option writing strategies in this book. It is important to stay focused. Minimise your choices and avoid confusion by mastering one skill before moving onto the next. As you gain proficiency in this field, you can commence option buying techniques.

Trading Secrets

Time is on your side as a writer. By writing option contracts, you will be involved in a trade with a high probability of success. You will have the power and control that a major underwriting corporation has in the warrants market!

To help you get the most out of this book, I would like to make a few suggestions. Perhaps you could think of me as your trading partner. As your partner, I will be totally frank with you about some of the things that I have done well, in addition to the mistakes that I have made trading options. Often one of the most cost-effective ways to learn is by using other people's experience, isn't it?

By putting in the effort to understand each topic before continuing reading, you will find that you will derive a greater understanding of writing options. Be patient with yourself and allow yourself the time required to learn a new, but very lucrative, skill. I am confident that you will not regret the effort you put in.

As I would like to see you do well in options, I have given you a number of exercises to complete throughout the book. By filling out the review sections set out after particularly significant chapters, you will have a chance to test your understanding of the concepts just covered. If there is any area that requires your attention to a greater degree, take the time to reread the chapter once or twice before moving on.

Included in many of the chapters are actual share charts. These illustrate my entry and exit points for some of the trades that I have conducted. I know the temptation is to skip over the examples. I have felt that temptation when reading many trading books myself. However, the best lessons can often be learned from studying actual trading situations. Even when the information in the charts is a few years old, the principles of analysis and action remain the same.

I have written this book with the assumption in mind that you are serious about making money and that you would like a practical 'guiding hand'. By taking the time to get the ideas in each chapter clear in your own mind, you will be ready to start making money in the options market by the time you finish reading this book.

Once you have fully understood the definitions of call and put options, you will find that the trading strategies will make a lot more sense. I have found that potential option writers find it most difficult to come to grips with the understanding of these definitions. Keep persisting and you will find that the meanings of these concepts will become clearer to you. Chapters 2 and 3 cover the definitions of call and put options. Below are some other basic definitions related to the options market. There is also a glossary at the back of the book.

BASIC TERMS

Here are some basic shares and options terms. Many of these terms will appear throughout this book, so you may need to refer to these pages and to the glossary from time to time.

Bearish View

This is a belief that the sharemarket, or a particular share, will decrease in value. If this is your view, you will be more likely to write call options. Locating a share which is trading in a sideways band is also considered bearish. In this situation, you could write both calls and puts. Obviously, I will go into these strategies in more detail in the following chapters.

Bullish View

This is a belief that the sharemarket or share will increase in value. If this is your view, you will be more likely to write put options.

Close-off

This is the expiration date, or final date, of the option contract. The close-off of each option contract is often up to 12 months, or more, from the time that it is issued. As a writer, you can choose to write contracts on options with any amount of time to expiry, e.g. six months to expiry, or one month to expiry. The choice is yours.

Contracts

Options are sold by the contract. One option contract usually covers 1000 shares. For example, five BHP options contracts would cover 5000 BHP shares. If BHP's share price was $16.00, this would mean that by writing five contracts, you would have exposure to $80,000 worth of BHP.

Defensive Actions

These are your last resort when the share goes against the view you had when you initially wrote the option. Defensive actions are a way of removing yourself from risk and minimising your loss if the trade goes against you.

Exercise

To exercise your rights as an option *buyer* means that the option has reached, or is close to, its strike price and you may exercise your *right* to buy or sell the shares covered by the option. You can do this at or before expiration. Only a minor percentage of options are actually exercised. Generally, options are traded as the premiums increase when the share trends in the expected direction. Option writers do not have the choice to initiate being exercised because they have the *obligations*, and the buyers have the *rights*. I will go into this in detail later.

Exchange-Traded Options

The options traded over shares in Australia are called 'exchange-traded options' or 'American-style options'. This type of option allows the option holder to exercise the option at any time during the life of the contract, up to and including the day of expiry.

Expiration

This is the final date of the option contract. In Australia, it is usually the last Thursday of every month, other than over the Christmas season. Technically the expiration date is the Thursday prior to the last trading Friday in the month. You can usually obtain a calendar of close-off dates from your broker or the Australian Stock Exchange (ASX).

Exposure

This is the total possible amount of money that you would be liable for as a writer if the options were to be exercised. This is a more critical concept when writing put options because if a significant downward correction occurs, it is likely that your written puts will be at risk.

Options Clearing House (OCH)

The OCH registers all option trades and maintains an orderly options market.

Premium

This is the price of the option. For example, you may receive a 30¢ premium when writing an option.

Strike Price

This is the price level at which you write your option contract. For example, you may receive a 30¢ premium when writing a call option at a $12.50 strike price.

Open Interest

This is the number of outstanding contracts at a particular strike price. It is a comparable concept to volume. It is essential as a writer and a buyer that you place your orders in liquid option positions, i.e. where there is a lot of open interest. Liquid positions are where there are many other buyers and sellers in the market. It is important that you do not trade in options with only a small trading volume each day. If you trade in these illiquid options, it may be difficult to exit these positions if the trade goes against you.

MAXIMISE YOUR SUCCESS IN TRADING OPTIONS

There are several key skills and attributes that are common amongst successful option traders:

- An emotionally objective mindset
- A good knowledge about options and defensive actions
- Good share analysis techniques
- An excellent administration system
- Soundly back-tested trading rules
- Reliable monitoring procedures
- Discipline.

If you do not know the flaws in your own personality, trading in the options market will reveal them to you!

This book will cover all of these areas, placing particular focus on options knowledge, share analysis, administration and rules for successful trading. For more information on how these areas relate to the sharemarket, as opposed to the options market, refer to one of my other books, *Trading Secrets*. In regard to discipline and the development of an objective mindset, I will discuss some of the key components related to these topics, but your own personal qualities of determination and persistence are of utmost importance. As with the majority of trading, your individual mindset is one of the most critical determinants of your success level.

Be aware that you should not act on the basis of any material in this book without considering, and taking, professional advice with due regard to your own circumstances. The decision to trade, and the method of trading or investing, is a personal decision and involves an inherent level of risk. Past performance is no guarantee of future profits, so you need to consider your decision to trade carefully, especially when becoming involved with a leveraged tool such as options.

➔   ➔   ➔   *Ever wondered how to make more money out of the shares that you own, and how to make money from a downtrending share? Keep reading to find out how by writing Call Options*   ➔   ➔   ➔

Chapter Two

WHAT ARE CALL

OPTIONS?

I n order to understand the options market, you need to consider the definition of an option from the perspective of the buyer as well as from the writer's perspective. Formal definitions of options tend to place emphasis on the buyer's view rather than the writer's view.

Definition

The formal definition of a call option from the buyer's perspective is as follows:

> *A call option gives the buyer the right to buy a given security at a certain price within a given time.*

Now, what does that really mean? Let me try to translate this into more easily understandable language. The buyer of a call option has the *right* (not obligation) to *buy* a given amount of the underlying security, on or before the expiry date, at a specified price. This specified price is called the 'strike price'. The buyer pays a certain amount of money to obtain these rights. This amount of money is called the 'premium'.

What You'll Find in the Newspaper

Both _The Australian_ and _The Australian Financial Review_ newspapers list option details. Call options appear in a separate section to put options.

In _The Australian_, you will find shares listed along with their previously recorded closing price. There is a column showing the expiry month and the strike prices for the options available for that month. The actual expiry dates and strike prices are set by the Australian Stock Exchange (ASX), so even though you are writing your own option contracts, you will generally need to conform to the strike prices that are detailed in the newspaper. All of the option tables shown in this text have been taken from _The Australian_.

Table 2.1 gives an example. Columns 3 and 4 show the buyer and seller prices. This is the spread of the demand from the buyers (who would like to buy a lower priced option), and the sellers (who would like to sell a higher priced option). The last sale is displayed, as well as the turnover and open interest at that particular strike price. The number of contracts trading at particular strike prices and for options of particular shares has important implications.

Table 2.1 OPTION INFORMATION

CALL OPTIONS

Stock	Strike Price	Buyer	Seller	Last Sale	T.O. 000	Open Int.
AMP Last Sale Price $16.20						
1999						
Jul	15.00	1.27	1.43	1.20		5
Jul	15.50	.88	1.02	1.00		81
Jul	16.00	.55	.65	.57	141	524
Jul	16.50	.32	.35	.30	12	431
Jul	17.00	.16	.19	.15	4	243
Jul	17.50	.06	.12	.09		160
Jul	18.00	.05	.08	.05	20	75

Source: _The Australian_

Depending on the newspaper, other information regarding options may also be listed. When writing options, I have found that the above information provides more than enough detail to conduct successful trades.

LIQUIDITY

I suggest that you only trade options that are liquid. Liquid means that there are many other people also trading that option, so you will have a large enough market to absorb supply and demand.

Options with low levels of trading are considered 'illiquid' and are best avoided. By trading in illiquid options, if the trade goes against you, exiting from your open positions will be considerably more difficult. Imagine being in a trade which is going against you, watching your profit erode with each passing hour, and being unable to act because there is an insufficient market available to allow you to exit from your position. This is a terrible scenario, but very common if you intend to deal in illiquid options.

"Options with low levels of trading are considered 'illiquid' and are best avoided."

The best protection from getting stuck in a losing trade is to trade only in liquid options and strike prices. Some traders will find it difficult to restrict their focus, as they feel that a brighter opportunity exists in shares that are not included in their narrow list of liquid options.

Personally, (at the time of writing this book), I write options only on the following stocks:

BHP (BHP)	**Commonwealth Bank (CBA)**	**News Corp (NCP)**
AMP (AMP)	**Western Mining (WMC)**	**Telstra (TLS)**
Rio Tinto (RIO)	**Lend Lease (LLC)**	**ANZ Bank (ANZ)**
Westpac Bank (WBC)	**National Australia Bank (NAB)**	

I have found that these options have sufficient volume and offer reasonable premiums.

Obviously over time, the liquidity of individual options will differ. I occasionally review the above list to ensure that there are significant levels of open interest available for these options. You will have to draw up your own short list and review it from time to time.

Some traders review the open interest section of the newspaper (given in the last column of Table 2.1) and trade only in strike prices that have above average volume levels. I prefer to take out the complexity that this step involves. If you would like to trade using this method, you will need to review each share option in general, as well as each strike price within that option. This is quite labour intensive, but many of the traders who take the time to perform this step swear by its effectiveness.

I prefer to add up the open interest levels available for each share and then trade options in those shares which have above average liquidity.

CALL OPTIONS — THE BUYER'S PERSPECTIVE

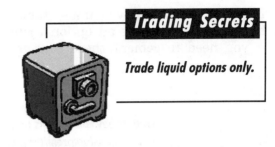

Trading Secrets

Trade liquid options only.

When option buyers believe that they have found a share that will trend upwards strongly, they buy a call option. They buy the option to secure their purchase of the share at a lower than market value if the market trends in the expected direction. Buyers may also trade the option as the share price increases. For example, they may buy an option for 30¢ and when it reaches 60¢, they may sell it for a 100% profit.

As a share goes up in value, the call option premium for that particular strike price increases. This is an essential principle which reveals why call option buyers profit from an uptrending share. The buyer can profit as long as the upward direction continues prior to the expiry date of the option. Because the buyer has bought a depreciating asset, this upward movement of the share must outweigh the time decay of the option in order to generate a profitable trade.

It is much easier to achieve a 100% profit with a leveraged tool, than by purchasing the underlying security. For example, imagine buying a $30.00 share and waiting for a 100% return! You may be waiting for a very long time indeed. It is quite feasible, however, to make a 100% return if you buy a call option at, say, 30¢. This is because a small increase in the price of the underlying share will have a multiplying effect on the value of the call option. It is this leveraged aspect of options that acts as a powerful magnet to option buyers.

Greed may be the predominant emotion for buyers. They may be thinking: 'Why would I buy a share at $30.00? Instead of buying the share, I could buy an option and have exposure to that share, but with a greater chance of making money! I could even double my money if everything goes my way. By crikey, that's what I'm going to do!'

Other option buyers may be dominated by fear. They may think that they will miss out on a winning opportunity unless they buy a call option. These buyers may be thinking: 'Hey, I'm pretty sure that this share is going to skyrocket in value. I would like to reserve some of those shares for myself at a lower than market value. If they do skyrocket, I have at least locked in my purchase price by buying these call options. My gosh, I'm getting more brilliant by the second!'

It is important that you understand the option buyer's motivation in order to trade effectively as an option writer. Take the time to review this section if you need to cement these concepts before moving on.

Trading Secrets

Traders buy call options on shares that are uptrending, hoping to profit from increasing premiums, or to lock in their purchase price at a lower than market value.

CALL OPTIONS — THE WRITER'S PERSPECTIVE

A call option writer has the obligation to sell a share to an option buyer. The writer collects a premium or fee from the option buyer and subsequently is obligated to fulfil the demands of the option buyer. Writers must sell their shares or have their shares called away from them, if the buyers decide to exercise their rights. This can occur at any time throughout the duration of the option contract.

"Defensive actions are designed to remove the writer from risk, even though a loss may be incurred."

If the writer has decided that he does not want to sell his shares, and that he would like to remove himself from the contract, there are several defensive actions that are available to him prior to being exercised.

Fear may be the predominant emotion for the writer. He may be thinking: 'I am happy with the paper profit I have made so far on this share. This bullish market cannot last much longer. Why don't I sell the share when it hits $15.00? This seems to be a fair price to sell. What I will do is write a call option over the shares that I own at $15.00. If the share hits this mark, I will be happy to have shares exercised at $15.00. By writing calls, I will get to keep the premium that I have written as well. What an astute business person I am!'

Greed may also enter the writer's heart. A call option writer who is trading for cash flow, rather than to lock in a sale price for his share, is usually of the opinion that the share will be trading in a sideways band, or be bearish in his view. He may think: 'if this share doesn't go past $10.00 within one month, I could make $500 by writing a call. An extra $500 sure would be handy...'

A major consideration of this whole discussion is the importance of rights and obligations. Imagine that you were the landlord of an apartment. When tenants pay you their rent, they are in a similar position to an option buyer. Because of this transaction, the landlord now has obligations to fulfil. (The landlord has taken the tenants' money just as the option writer has taken the option buyer's money.) The landlord must make sure that the plumbing is kept in working order, and that the hot water system is functional. The landlord has an obligation to supply this to the tenant. The tenant has the right to expect this from the landlord as the tenant has paid his rent in good faith. In the same way, the buyer of the option has all of the rights and the writer of the option maintains obligations. The writer forfeited his rights as soon as he accepted the monetary premium from the option buyer.

Trading Secrets

▸ *Traders write call options on sideways or downtrending shares or over shares that they own to benefit from the premiums that they receive.*

▸ *Buyers have rights. Writers have obligations.*

An Example

Let's have a look at an example. The charts shown in this book will be candlestick charts. These charts differ in appearance from the bar charts that you may be used to seeing. Chapter 6, Candlestick Secrets will provide you with a more detailed understanding about how to interpret these charts.

If you wrote an AMP call option at $17.00, (see Fig. 2.1 overleaf), and the current price was $16.00, you would be of the view that AMP would not go above the $17.00 mark. If you, the call option writer, are correct, and AMP stayed below the $17.00 point, you would then keep the premium that the buyer had paid you.

The option buyers would be of the view that AMP would move up to, say, $18.00 — giving them the ability to buy the share for $17.00 — a profit of $1.00 per share (if we disregard transaction costs). Buyers could choose to exercise their rights and buy the share at $17.00 or benefit from the increasing option premiums as the share price increases.

FIG. 2.1 AMP DAILY

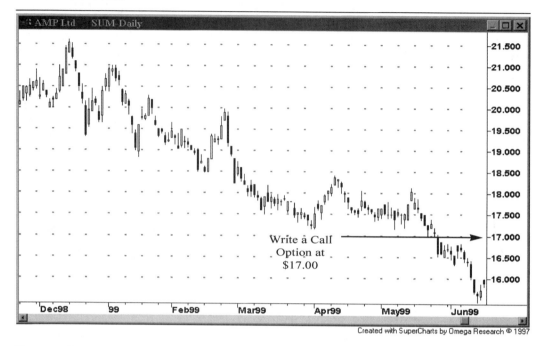

Buyers have the rights in this relationship. They have the right to exercise their option and purchase the share from the writer, at the agreed price at or before the expiry date. Buyers can exercise their rights even prior to the share reaching the strike price.

As a share goes up in value, the call option premium for that particular strike price also increases. This is an essential principle which reveals why call option buyers profit from an uptrending share. Buyers can profit as long as the direction continues (in excess of the effects of time decay) and they sell their option to attain this profit.

If the share price stays below the strike price of the contract, then the premium received by the writer is usually retained in full. The option will expire worthless at the expiry date of the contract, as the writer initially sold the buyer a depreciating asset. The majority of bought options expire worthless. For this reason, time is on the side of the writer and, in fact, the writer may be considered to be selling the time decay of the option.

TYPES OF CALL OPTIONS

There are two main types of call options: covered calls (or scrip-covered calls) and naked calls.

Covered Call or Scrip Covered Call Options

This is where you own the underlying stock and you write calls over this stock. If you are exercised, and you have written a call with a strike price greater than your purchase price, you will realise a capital gain on the share, in addition to the premium that you received for writing the call. This is definitely the best way to start out in the options market if you already own shares.

Be aware, however, that you must only write options against shares that you are willing to sell or you will need to take defensive actions to remove yourself from risk before being exercised. Defensive actions are discussed in Chapter 9, Defending Your Turf.

Naked Call Options

This is where you write a call when you do not own the stock. It is totally innocent... really...

Using a naked call strategy will allow you to write a greater number of option contracts if your financial resources are limited, as you do not have to own vast quantities of shares (although you will have to provide a small amount of cash or shares to cover margin requirements—this is discussed in greater detail in Chapter 12).

It is important to understand that when writing naked call options, technically your loss is unlimited. Although this sounds terrifying, in practice, this risk is not as sombre as it first appears. There are ways to minimise the risk and remove yourself from the risk altogether by taking defensive actions. The reason why the loss is considered unlimited is due to the chance occurrence that the underlying security will skyrocket to an astronomical value without any warning whatsoever. With careful monitoring and the application of technical analysis, the risk can be calculated and minimised.

Whenever I write an options contract that is not covered by shares that I already own, I am always pleased when the contract expires worthless. This is my whole aim when writing naked call options.

Trading Secrets

▸ *A cautious way to start writing options is to write calls over shares that you already own. This is called writing a covered call.*

▸ *A naked call is a call option written over a share that you do not own.*

Terminology

It is essential that you use the correct terminology when speaking to your broker or you may be held personally liable for any errors! This can be an extremely costly mistake.

When you initially open your written positions, you actually receive money from the option buyer. Just imagine that you were selling a bicycle for $200. The buyer of the bicycle would hand you the money and you would put the $200 in your pocket. Just as you sold the bicycle and received money, when you write an option, you will receive money. For this reason, to open a written option position, you actually 'Sell to Open' a position.

When writing options, you receive a set amount of money that is held in trust and is deposited into your bank account when the options expire worthless. Usually when purchasing shares, you are in the habit of paying money to complete the transaction. When writing options, you receive money.

Here is the exact terminology required when you initially enter a written call option position:

To open a position:	Sell to open 5 BHP September 'xx $19.00 call contracts at 40¢.

This order is clearly an option *writing* trade as you are *selling to open the transaction*. The five signifies the number of contracts that you are writing. As you will remember, five contracts cover 5000 BHP shares, and the expiry month is September. The 'xx denotes the year, for example these options may expire in the year 2000. The strike price is $19.00 and you are writing call options. The premium that you will receive from this transaction is 40¢ per share for every contract written.

Trading Secrets

Always use the correct terminology when placing your option orders. Your broker is not a mind reader.

REVIEW

1) Imagine that you do not own any shares whatsoever. If you believe that a particular share is trading in a sideways band and that there is a chance that it could break downwards, what type of option would you write?

_____

_____

2) Write down the correct terminology you would need to use to write three call options over BHP due for expiry in March 'xx at a strike price of $20.00 and a premium value of 50¢.

_____

_____

ANSWERS

1) A covered call option is written over shares that you own to maximise the return on your investment. Another alternative is to write a naked call where you do not own the shares but do have deposits with your broker. If you have detected a share that is trending downwards or in a sideways band, and you do not own any shares, you are most likely to write a naked call option.

2) Sell to open 3 BHP March 'xx $20.00 call contracts at 50¢.

(Obviously the examples of terminology used throughout this book are entirely contrived and not intended to provide any indication as to the actual premiums that you can obtain when writing a contract such as this.)

➔ ➔ ➔ _Are you interested in making even more money out of an uptrending share? Then the next chapter is definitely essential reading!_ ➔ ➔ ➔

Chapter Three

WHAT ARE PUT OPTIONS?

PUT OPTIONS — THE BUYER'S PERSPECTIVE

L et's consider put options from the perspective of the buyer.
A put option gives the buyer the right to sell a given security at a certain price within a given time.

The buyer of a put option has the right (not obligation) to sell a given amount of the underlying security, on or before the expiry date, at a specified price. In other words, buyers put their shares to the writers if they exercise their contracts. Put option buyers are bearish in their view. The purchase of put options is commonly used as an insurance policy on shares. The buyer may buy a put option with a strike price below the current market price. If the share trends downwards strongly, the option will allow the buyer to sell his shares at a higher than market value. So put option buyers either buy the option to secure the sale of the share at a higher than market value, or to profit from the increasing premiums when the share trends down.

As a share goes down in value, the put option premium for that particular strike price increases. This is an essential principle which reveals why put option buyers profit from a downtrending share. The buyer can profit as long as the downward direction continues prior to the expiry date (in excess of the effects of time decay). If the share trends in a sideways band, both call option buyers and put option buyers will lose money due to the effects of time decay. The share needs to trend strongly in the expected direction to generate profit.

Some put option buyers may be thinking: 'I'm pretty sure the share that I've just bought will go up in value immediately, but what if it doesn't? I'm going to feel like an idiot. What I am going to do is buy a put option at 50¢ below the current share price. If the share drops in value dramatically, I will be able to sell the share at a loss of only 50¢ (excluding premium and transaction costs). If I do not lock in my sale price, my potential loss could be a great deal more than only 50¢! Buying a put is like purchasing insurance on my portfolio. I'm happy to pay a bit of insurance money that will provide me with protection in case a significant share price dip occurs'.

"If the share trends in a sideways band, both call option buyers and put option buyers will lose money due to the effects of time decay."

Other put option buyers may think: 'Hey, the market is totally overheated, and a correction is due. If this share drops in value, I could make a pile of money by buying puts. The more it goes down, the more money I'll make on my puts!'

Trading Secrets

Traders buy put options on shares that are downtrending to profit from increasing premiums or to lock in a share sale price at a higher than market value.

PUT OPTIONS — THE WRITER'S PERSPECTIVE

Put option writers are usually of the opinion that the share will be trading in a sideways band, or they are bullish in their view. They are under obligation to buy the shares from a put option taker should they be exercised.

The writer is probably thinking: 'There is no way that this share will go down in value! I am definite it will stay above $10.00. I'm going to write a put with a strike price of $10.00, and keep the premium the buyer will pay me. I know I'm right about this one!'

Alternatively, the writer may think: 'I reckon it would be OK to buy this share for $9.00, but if I do not buy it at all, it doesn't really worry me. I think I will write a put with a strike price of $9.00 and keep the premium that I'll be paid. If it stays above $9.00 then I won't buy it. However, if I end up buying it at $9.00 that sounds like fair value to me. Either way I'll be happy.'

Trading Secrets

Traders write put options on sideways or uptrending shares to benefit from the premiums that they receive or to purchase a share at a set price.

AN EXAMPLE

Imagine that you wrote a CBA put option with a strike price of $26.00, (see Fig. 3.1), and the current price was $28.00. You would be of the view that CBA would not go below the $26.00 mark. If you are correct, and CBA stayed above the $26.00 point, you would then keep the premium that the taker had paid. The option buyer would be of the view that CBA would downtrend strongly past the $26.00 point, and stop at the $25.00 mark, for example. This would give him the ability to put his shares to you for $26.00 even though the share may be priced at $25.00 and take a profit of $1.00 per share (excluding premium and transaction costs). If the put option taker was correct, he could sell the option prior to expiry and make a profit on his premium, or exercise his option and sell his shares at $26.00.

As with the discussion of call options, the writer has the obligations, and the buyer has the rights in the relationship. Put option buyers have the right to exercise their contracts on or before the expiry date, as well as prior to the share downtrending past the strike price.

If the share price stays above the strike price of the put contract, then the premium received by the writer is usually retained in full. The option then expires worthless at the expiry date of the contract. For this reason, time is on the side of the writer. The writer may be considered to be selling the time decay of the option. We will discuss the relevance of time decay in more detail in the next chapter.

Fɪɢ. 3.1 COMMONWEALTH BANK DAILY

Created with SuperCharts by Omega Research © 1997

Although there are defensive actions that can be implemented to limit the risk, you must remember that when writing options, technically the loss is unlimited. It is for this reason that regular monitoring of all your open positions is an essential component of trading options.

Trading Secrets

The threat of an unexpected market crash means that written puts have inherently more risk than written calls.

TERMINOLOGY

Using the correct terminology when opening and closing positions is essential. By always using the correct wording, your broker will be more likely to understand your intentions. Here is the correct wording to open a position when writing put options:

"Using the correct terminology when opening and closing positions is essential."

To open a position:	**Sell to open 5 BHP August 'xx $13.00 put contracts at 10¢.**

KNOW YOUR PLAYERS

From the discussion above, you will start to gain an insight into the motivations of both buyers and sellers of options. It is essential that you know the players in the market, particularly when there are situations that will influence their behaviour. By looking at these areas of vested interest you can more accurately assess the level of risk to which you are exposed.

The next section summarises options from the perspective of the buyer and the writer using some tables for illustration. Make sure you have firmly grasped the differences.

SUMMARY FROM THE BUYER'S PERSPECTIVE

Call Option Buying

Call option buyers are seeking shares that have a high probability of increasing in value, (see Table 3.1). If their view is incorrect and the share goes down in value, it is possible for them to lose all of their capital invested in that trade. (Of course, they could extricate themselves from the trade prior to this.) They cannot lose more than the amount of the capital that they dedicated to the option purchase. For this reason, buyers have an automatic limit when considering their potential total loss. This perceived limited risk often encourages complete novices to enter the options buying arena. However, when you examine the probabilities of a successful trade, writing options is the superior strategy as 85% of options are not exercised.

Novice buyers of options are particularly attracted to cheap options, which ironically have very little probability of generating a profit. Just as many families still gamble on the small probability of winning Tattslotto, there is a very slim chance that this will ever happen. The slight probability that they will actually win is overcome by the small amount of money required for a Tattslotto ticket, and this seems irresistible and worth the gamble. These reasons assist in explaining why a vast majority of option buyers end up net losers in the market. Buyers of low priced options make a trade where the rewards are potentially high, but there is a low probability of this trade being successful.

If the buyers' view is correct and the share increases in value, they could either sell the option at a profit, or if they chose, they could exercise their rights. They would have the right to purchase the writer's shares at the strike price (which will represent a lower than market value).

Put Option Buying

Put option buyers are seeking shares that have a high probability of decreasing in value, (see Table 3.1). If their view is incorrect and the share goes up considerably in value, it is possible for them to lose all of their capital invested in that trade. (Of course, they could extricate themselves from the trade prior to this happening.) They cannot lose more than the amount of the capital that they dedicated to the option purchase, so they have an automatic upper limit when considering their potential total loss. This contrasts to the technically unlimited loss that you are facing as an option writer for calls or puts.

TABLE 3.1 SUMMARY FROM THE BUYER'S PERSPECTIVE

	Call Option Buyer	Put Option Buyer
View	Bullish	Bearish
If view was wrong	Lose our capital/ Defensive action	Lose our capital/ Defensive action
If view was correct	SELL option at a profit	SELL option at a profit
If we exercise	We BUY shares below current market value	We SELL shares above current market value

If the bearish view of a put option buyer is correct and the share decreases in value, he could choose from two courses of action. Either he could sell the option at a profit, or if he chose to exercise his rights, he could sell his shares at the strike price (which will represent a higher than market value).

SUMMARY FROM THE WRITER'S PERSPECTIVE

Call Option Writing

A call option writer usually has a bearish view or a belief that the share will trend sideways, (see Table 3.2). This is especially true if naked calls are being written. If this view is not fulfilled by the behaviour of the share, and the strike price of the call is threatened, the writer must sell his shares at the specified strike price. There is a range of defensive actions that can be implemented, if necessary, in order to reduce the risk of this happening.

"...time decay is a critical aspect. The writer has sold the buyer a depreciating asset."

If the share price is below the strike price on the expiry date, the writer's sideways to bearish view has been fulfilled. Therefore, the writer keeps the premium paid by the option buyer. In terms of reward and probability, option writers make trades with a high probability of success, where the rewards are known in advance because they receive a fixed premium that cannot differ in value after the option is written.

Put Option Writing

A put option writer usually has a bullish view or a belief that the share will continue trending sideways, (see Table 3.2). If his view is not fulfilled by the behaviour of the share, it is likely that the option will be exercised. If the option is exercised, the writer must buy shares at the specified strike price. The option buyer has the right to exercise his contracts whenever the spirit moves him. Unless the strike price is close to the share price, however, it is unlikely that the buyer will have any vested interest in exercising. Defensive actions are available to prevent this ultimate obligation to purchase shares and it may be preferable to take defensive action rather than be exercised.

TABLE 3.2 SUMMARY FROM THE WRITER'S PERSPECTIVE

	Call Option Writer	Put Option Writer
View	Sideways/Bearish	Sideways/Bullish
If view was wrong	Defensive action	Defensive action
If exercised	Must SELL shares below current market value	Must BUY shares above current market value
At expiry if view correct	Keep premium	Keep premium
What we are selling	Time decay	Time decay

If the share price is above the strike price on the expiry date, the writer's sideways to bullish view has been fulfilled by the share's price activity. Consequently, the writer keeps the premium paid by the option buyer in full.

Time decay is a critical aspect. Time is on the side of the writer as he has sold the buyer a depreciating asset.

Take some time to read over the definitions in this chapter. It is only by understanding these issues that you can move on to a more detailed discussion about option strategies. The definitions of call options and put options are probably the most difficult concepts to grasp when you are beginning to learn about this market. Your understanding will grow in direct proportion to the amount of effort that you exert. Your efforts will be well rewarded in profits!

Trading Secrets

Whenever you are writing or buying options, it is wise to keep in mind 'What's in it for the other guy?' The option buyer has an opposing view to the writer, and will stand to gain if his view is fulfilled. Remember this prior to plunging into a trade which 'couldn't possibly go wrong'.

REVIEW

1) If your view of a share is bullish (i.e. you think the share is going up), what type of option would you *write*?

_____

2) If your view of a share is bullish, what type of option would you *buy*?

_____

3) If your view of a share is bearish (i.e. you think the share is going down), what type of option would you *write*?

_____

4) If your view of a share is bearish, what type of option would you *buy*?

_____

5) What is the correct terminology if you would like to write five put options on BHP due for expiry in November 2000 at a strike price of $12.00 and a premium value of 20¢?

_____

ANSWERS

1) You would be inclined to write put options if your view is bullish.
2) You would buy call options if your view is bullish.
3) If your view is bearish, you would write call options.
4) If your view is bearish, you would buy put options.
5) Sell to open 5 BHP November 2000 $12.00 put contracts at 20¢.

➔ ➔ ➔ *Would you like to know how to estimate the theoretical value of options to make sure you're getting a good deal? The next chapter will help you to become a bargain hunter in the options market* ➔ ➔ ➔

THE PRICING

PUZZLE

Many factors have a large impact on the price of an option. It is critical to come to an understanding of these factors in order to determine whether an option represents 'fair value' to trade. These factors also have an impact on the cost and timing of the defensive actions that you may consider taking if the trade turns against you.

Algebra and I have not been the best of companions over the years. Rather than provide you with a revolting array of mathematical formulae, I would like to show you some general principles that impact upon the premium value of an option.

Option pricing models are available to help calculate the theoretical premium value of options at specific strike prices. One of the difficulties with these models is that if the derived price is not backed by market support, then you have gone to a lot of effort to calculate a figure that is largely useless. I prefer to let the market dictate the fair value based on the following concepts.

THE DEGREE OF RISK

As a general rule, the greater the risk, the greater the potential reward. This definitely holds true when referring to the sharemarket.

The proximity of the strike price to the share price is a major consideration. In order to understand this, a discussion of in-the-money, at-the-money, and out-of-the-money is essential.

"The greater the risk, the greater the potential reward."

I will be covering this concept from the view of the buyer as well as the writer. If you find that alternating between buying and writing strategies is confusing, then skip over the text related to buying strategies. Once you have become more familiar with the terminology, you can review the buyer's perspective with more clarity.

IN-THE-MONEY

A call option is said to be in-the-money when the current stock price is above the strike price. A put option that has the current stock price below the strike price is also in-the-money. Have a look at these LLC examples in Fig. 4.1 and Fig. 4.2, to gain a greater understanding of this principle.

FIG. 4.1 CALL OPTION STRIKE PRICES

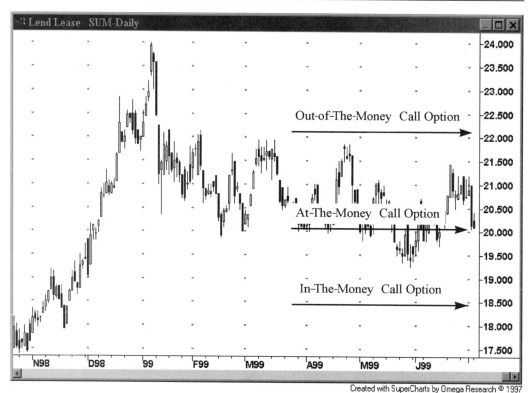

Created with SuperCharts by Omega Research ® 1997

FIG. 4.2 PUT OPTION STRIKE PRICES

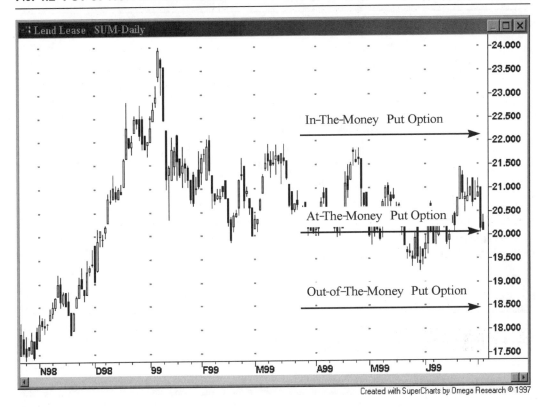

Created with SuperCharts by Omega Research © 1997

The price of the option is made up of the intrinsic value plus the time value. The intrinsic value is the difference between the market value of the share and the strike price of the option. For example, if the option is $2.00 in-the-money, the price of the option will be $2.00 plus the time value (see Fig. 4.3 and Fig. 4.4 overleaf).

To *buy* an in-the-money option with some intrinsic value is a conservative strategy. It already has some inherent value over and above the time value that you are purchasing. Your initial purchase price for the option will be higher than if you followed a more aggressive strategy, but it represents a safer alternative.

To *write* an in-the-money option is an aggressive strategy which will attract a very high premium. However, you must have a clear view that the share will trend in the direction that will ensure that the option will become out-of-the-money by the expiry date or you will, (in all probability), be exercised.

FIG. 4.3 CALL OPTIONS AND INTRINSIC VALUE

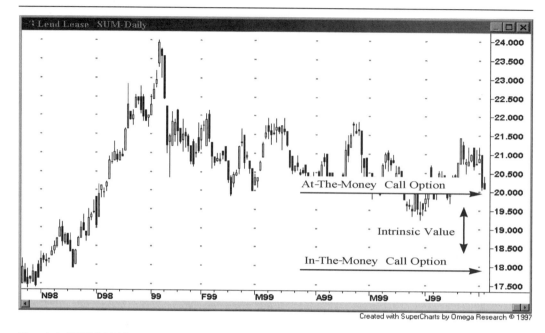

Created with SuperCharts by Omega Research ® 1997

FIG. 4.4 PUT OPTIONS AND INTRINSIC VALUE

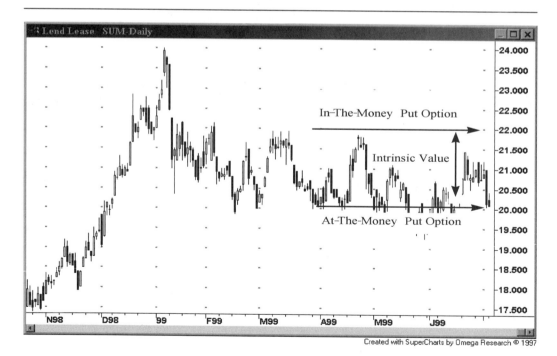

Created with SuperCharts by Omega Research ® 1997

Writing an in-the-money put option is more dangerous than writing an in-the-money call option. This is because there is a vested interest by the buyer of the put option to exercise, as well as the threat of a market downturn. Exercising a put contract early will enable the buyer to free up his capital by selling his shares to the option writer. Call options are more likely to be exercised at, or close to, expiry.

In addition, you need to be aware of the effect of dividends on the buyer's level of vested interest to exercise. Initially avoid writing in-the-money call and put options, especially if the share will be going ex-dividend prior to the expiry date.

DELTA

The deeper in-the-money an option becomes, the more likely the delta of the option will become 1:1. The delta is the sensitivity of option price to changes in share price. For example, if a delta is 0.70, for every $1 in share price increase, the option premium will increase by 70¢ Therefore, if you buy an option that is worth 70¢, you will approximately double your money when the underlying share increases in price by $1. This explains why it is best to take prompt action if a trade turns against you.

Personally, I do not focus on the delta when initiating written option strategies, so if you are uncertain about the impact of this concept, don't be too concerned. It is only when buying options that the delta assumes greater significance.

Trading Secrets

▸ *Writing in-the-money options is an aggressive strategy, especially when writing puts.*

▸ *As the option becomes deeper in-the-money, the delta will become closer to 1:1. This higher delta has the effect of costing you more money to extricate yourself from a written losing position. For this reason, it is best to avoid letting your options become too deeply in-the-money prior to taking a defensive action.*

AT-THE-MONEY

Options are said to be at-the-money when the strike price of the option approximately matches the share price.

To *buy* at-the-money options is a fairly aggressive strategy. You must have a clear view that the share will trend in the direction that will ensure that the option will become in-the-money in order to benefit from trading the option as the premium increases. It may not be feasible for a buyer to exercise an at-the-money option due to brokerage costs required to buy or sell the shares covered by the option.

In my view, only short-term option buying strategies should implement an at-the-money trading position. Short-term at-the-money positions may represent an acceptable degree of risk. There is usually a large market available for at-the-money options whether you are buying or selling.

To *write* an at-the-money option is an aggressive strategy that attracts good high premiums. You must have a clear view that the share will trend in the direction that will ensure that the option will become out-of-the-money by the expiry date or you will, in all probability, be exercised. Your analysis has to approach perfection for this strategy to be effective. You have left yourself no room for error, and your stress levels will no doubt reflect this fact until the written option becomes out-of-the-money.

Trading Secrets

If you are learning about options, I suggest that you avoid writing in-the-money and at-the-money options. It is important that you focus on conservative strategies initially.

OUT-OF-THE-MONEY

A call option is said to be out-of-the-money when the current share price is *below* the strike price. Similarly, a put option is out-of-the-money when the current share price is *above* the strike price.

To *buy* an out-of-the-money option is the most aggressive strategy available. The option contains no intrinsic value and is all time value.

To *write* an out-of-the-money option is a conservative strategy. It will attract reasonable premiums although the premiums will be much less than those available at strike prices that are in- or at-the-money. The further out-of-the-money the option strike price, the lower the premium value.

Writing out-of-the-money options will minimise the amount of risk to which you are exposed. This strategy provides you with a margin for error. If the share does not trend in the direction you are hoping, you are still removed slightly from the risk. If your timing is slightly incorrect, and the share does trend in the expected direction after a certain period of time, by writing an out-of-the-money option, your chances of having your strike price threatened are lessened.

Because the time decay curve is on the writer's side, it is possible to slightly miscalculate the direction of the share, and still break-even on the trade. For example, the share may go down in value temporarily prior to continuing its uptrend. For your written call options, as long as the share price remains below the strike price by the expiry date, you are usually safe and it is unlikely that you will be exercised. For your written put options, as long as the share price remains above the strike price by the expiry date, it is unlikely that you will be exercised.

To summarise, if you are looking to follow a conservative strategy, you would purchase in-the-money options and write out-of-the-money options, (see Table 4.1).

TABLE 4.1 CONSERVATIVE vs AGGRESSIVE STRATEGIES

	Conservative	Aggressive
WRITE	Out-of-the-Money Calls and Puts	At- and In-the-Money Calls and Puts
BUY	In-the-Money Calls and Puts	At- and Out-of-the-Money Calls and Puts

TESTING, TESTING

It is time to test your knowledge. Fill out Table 4.2 and state whether the option is in-, out-of- or at-the-money. The answers are at the end of the chapter in Table 4.3.

TABLE 4.2 IN-, OUT-OF- OR AT-THE-MONEY STRIKE PRICES

Share Price	Strike Price	Call or Put	In-, Out-of- or At-the-Money
$9.00	$8.50	Call	_____
$9.00	$8.50	Put	_____
$9.00	$9.00	Put	_____
$9.00	$9.50	Call	_____
$9.00	$9.75	Put	_____

Trading Secrets

The closer the share price is to your option strike price, the higher the premium and the greater the risk to the writer.

VOLATILITY OF THE SHARE

The more volatile the share, the higher the option premium price. A simple way to see the effect of volatility is to examine a share chart. The days that have higher volatility or bar length are the days that attract a higher premium. Choppy shares with greater distances from the peak to the trough of the share price action are more volatile and will attract higher premiums. For shares with a lower volatility level, the option premiums will also be lower.

Traditionally, as sharemarkets have reached record levels in the past and have had a few sharp corrections, investor perception of the market is that a fall could be imminent. What has gone up, must come down! Each minor fall erodes investor confidence that the current lofty levels cannot be maintained. The options market provides a form of insurance and thus peace of mind for investors.

Investors buy puts to insure their portfolio with an automatic stop loss. Traders look to buy puts to benefit from downtrending securities, so if there is a threat of a downward correction, puts automatically become very attractive. When a large number of people are buying a particular instrument, the price of that instrument is likely to increase (as demand is outstripping supply).

As puts become more costly when there is the threat of a downward correction, the price of call options automatically increases, as they are two halves of the same coin. Another reason for the price of call options to rise in value is that buying calls requires the initial outlay to be only a fraction of the investment required to buy a share. This provides an incentive to buy calls for uptrending shares, instead of buying the underlying security. In times of volatility, traders may wish to limit their financial exposure to the market by buying options.

In these conditions, options become more expensive across the board. This is the appeal of *writing* calls and puts in periods of volatility! There is a primed market to purchase options and liquidity becomes less of an issue. In addition, the premiums you receive are markedly higher. What a terrific combination for option writers. An understanding of historic and implied volatility will be necessary as your options trading skills develop.

Trading Secrets

Periods of higher volatility are to be coveted by the option writer. The more sophisticated traders <u>sell</u> options in periods of high volatility and <u>buy</u> options in periods of low volatility.

TIME DECAY

The longer an option has until maturity, the greater the time value reflected in the price of the premium, (see Fig. 4.5). For example, a December option will incur a higher premium than a November option in the same year.

Have you ever felt, the older you get, the quicker time seems to rush by? Well, to a large extent, options react in the same way. Options lose value at an ever-increasing rate as they move towards the expiry date (when all else remains equal, e.g. price of the share, volatility, etc.). Figure 4.5 refers to the entire life of the option. As is evident, the closer the option is to expiry, the more steeply the curve slopes.

The relationship of option value to time is exponential, not linear in nature. By exponential I mean that the effect of time decay is not consistent throughout the life of the option. The time decay curve is flat at the beginning of an option's life and accelerates downwards towards the expiry date of the option.

Fig. 4.5 THE TIME DECAY CURVE

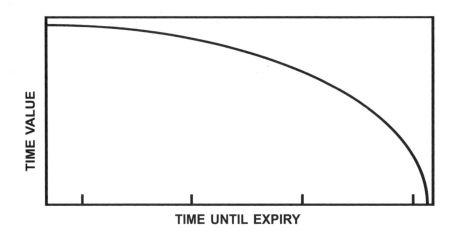

As a *buyer* of an option it is prudent to purchase an option with several months time value before the expiry date in order to avoid the exponential section of the time decay curve. For a buyer who would like to trade for increased premiums as the share trends, it is wise to exit the trade at least one month before expiry.

For writers of options, this time decay curve demonstrates the rationale behind writing options with less than, say, four weeks to expiry, as this is when the time premium is falling quickly.

When writing or buying options you must carefully balance the effect of time with the level or risk you are prepared to accept. For example, it may be possible for you to guess what the price of a particular share will be in four weeks time. Depending on your skill level, there is a good chance that this educated guess could result in being pretty close to the actual share price. However, if you tried to estimate what the share price would be in two years time, this would present a much more difficult challenge. There is a higher level of risk involved in trying to estimate what a share price will be in two years time, compared to trying to estimate what the share price will be in four weeks. This higher level of risk for longer-term estimations results in a higher premium value.

Trading Secrets

Time decay is also active over the weekend, so write shorter-term options on a Friday and maximise the decay in your favour.

OTHER INFLUENCES

There are many other influences upon option pricing. Although it is interesting to consider these influences, when you are starting to trade options it is *not* essential to analyse them all. It is not even necessary to understand every definition in order to trade options effectively. I find that if I get too side-tracked with details, I miss many trading opportunities.

Listed below are some of the other factors affecting option prices:

Theta — Sensitivity of the option price to the passing of time.

Gamma — Sensitivity of the delta to changes in share price.

Vega — Sensitivity of the option price to a change in share price volatility.

Iota — Sensitivity of the option price to interest rate changes.

REVIEW

1) How would you describe an in-the-money put?

_____

2) What is an out-of-the-money call?

_____

3) If you would like a conservative option writing strategy, would you write in-the-money options?

_____

4) What are the most important factors influencing the premium value of an option?

_____

_____

ANSWERS

1) An in-the-money put option is where the share price of the option is located below the strike price. If you have started out by writing an out-of-the-money put option, the option will become in-the-money when the share price drops through the strike price. Writing in-the-money puts is a very risky strategy as there is a high probability that you will be exercised. Put options are more likely than call options to be exercised prior to expiry.

2) An out-of-the-money call is where the strike price is above the current share price.

3) No. A conservative strategy is to write out-of-the-money options. Writing out-of-the-money calls is generally more conservative than writing out-of-the-money puts.

4) There are several factors influencing the premium value of the option. Of these, the most important are the degree of risk, volatility and time decay.

TABLE 4.3 IN-, OUT-OF- OR AT-THE-MONEY STRIKE PRICES

Share Price	Strike Price	Call or Put	In-, Out-of- or At-the-Money
$9.00	$8.50	Call	In-the-money
$9.00	$8.50	Put	Out-of-the-money
$9.00	$9.00	Put	At-the-money
$9.00	$9.50	Call	Out-of-the-money
$9.00	$9.75	Put	In-the-money

→   →   →   *Want to know some simple techniques to maximise your option premiums and put more money in your pocket? Read on...*

Chapter Five

ANALYTICAL

EXCELLENCE_

There are several excellent books on the finer points of technical analysis. My goal in this chapter is not to re-create these works, but to give you an insight into which of the techniques I utilise in forming a view on a share, prior to trading in options. I would like to give you a quick reference guide that you can use to refine your option analysis techniques.

If you are a mechanic, you probably need some specific tools to help you do your job. You could try loosening a nut with your fingers alone, but you wouldn't get very far. The technical and fundamental indicators provide you with tools to assist in analysing a share. Your skill will determine your success in forecasting the future direction of a share.

One of the best texts on the subject of analysis is _The Art of Trading_ by Christopher Tate. This provides an excellent basis for any of your technical analysis endeavours.

TECHNICAL ANALYSIS VS FUNDAMENTAL ANALYSIS

Technical analysis looks at the past price and volume action of the share to predict future performance. By using indicators that have been tested over time, trends can be determined to assist in forecasting future share price action. The technical analyst can then devise strategies to make money based on this analysis.

I follow a simple system of technical analysis based on just a few tried and true indicators. I suggest that you review my techniques, but if you have something that is already working for you, stick with that methodology! Remember to keep in mind the duration of your view on the share. A medium-term investor with a six-month time horizon will have a different view than a short-term (one week to three months) trader.

"Fundamental analysis should not be used exclusively in options trading. "

Technical analysis will answer the question *'when should I purchase?'* based on the share chart and indicators. Fundamental analysis assists in detecting *which* shares have a probability of increasing or decreasing in value based on the company balance sheet and profit and loss details.

In my view, fundamental analysis should not be used exclusively in options trading. The timing tools provided by technical analysis will maximise your premiums, assist in determining a strike price, and detect short-term trends within the overall longer-term trend.

The other type of analysis that you could try is reading newspapers and listening to rumours, opinion and hearsay. Your neighbours, friends and favourite journalist may mean well, but it is unlikely that they will suffer any consequences if you act on the strength of their opinion. This popular, but exceptionally unproductive technique, is the way that most people buy and sell shares. Headlines in newspapers directly feed their greed and fear, and these sources often display unsubstantiated views about the direction that a share will take. Unless you would like to create a small fortune (after starting with a large fortune), do *not* be tempted to take your advice from these sources.

Personally, I *never* give tips, and I *never* listen to tips. When I hold a training course, I teach people how to analyse share performance for themselves. I have found that trading on information received in the form of a 'hot tip' is unpredictable and foolhardy. Amateurs *react* emotionally. Professionals

"I never give tips and I never listen to tips."

consider carefully the implications of their actions prior to responding. The next time someone rushes up to tell you about the latest 'sure thing', take the time to review a share chart to see whether their recommendation makes technical sense.

Stan Weinstein's book on *Secrets for Profiting in Bull and Bear Markets* puts forward a terrific philosophy on trading shares. He states:

"1. *Never buy or sell a stock without checking the chart.*

2. *Never buy a stock when good news comes out, especially if the chart shows a significant advance prior to the news release.*

3. *Never buy a stock because it appears cheap after getting smashed. When it sells off further, you'll find out that cheap can become far cheaper!*

4. *Never buy a stock in a downtrend on the chart.*

5. *Never hold a stock that is in a downtrend, no matter how low the price/ earnings ratio. Many weeks later and several points lower, you'll find out why the stock was going down.*

6. *Always be consistent. If you find that you're sometimes buying, sometimes selling in practically identical situations, then there is something terribly wrong with your discipline.*"

These principles are based on purchasing shares as a strategy, but it pays to keep these concepts in mind when trading options.

Is it Necessary to Have a Charting Software Package?

Is it important for scuba divers to take a tank of oxygen with them when they dive? Only if they want to stay alive.

Yes, it is essential to have a software package to help you chart the share prices and perform different analyses. If you are not in a position to have access to a charting package, perhaps you should place your option trading on hold until you can set yourself up with the correct equipment. While it is possible to trade shares without a software package, I suggest that a computer is essential in order to trade options effectively.

My Approach

Here is the methodology that I use to analyse a share:

⮑   Firstly, I review the overall market direction as measured by the weekly All Ordinaries Index.

⮑   Secondly, I review a weekly chart of the appropriate index to gain an understanding of the overall trend for that industry.

⮑   Then I look at the weekly and daily chart of the share that I have chosen to write options over.

I use the weekly chart to determine the overall trend and the daily chart to see the short-term trends within the major trend. By staying true to the medium-term trend and the short-term trends, I stack the deck in my favour in terms of detecting a trade with a high probability of success.

It is important that you know the term of your investment decision. Because the majority of my trades are short-term in nature (usually I am in and out within approximately four weeks), I tend to rely on short-term indicators to time my entry and exit points. I rely on the medium-term indicators to assist me in detecting the overall direction of the trend. Using these indicators I can maximise the premiums that I receive.

Without a charting package to assist in these activities, I would be forced to draw charts by hand and waste limitless hours. Imagine trying to plot on paper a daily and weekly set of charts on BHP and its appropriate index! Why not let a computer number-crunch, so that you can be set free to trade effectively?

Changes in Behaviour

I like to think of each share as a child who exhibits certain personality characteristics. Some children breeze through their school years and get straight As. They never give their parents a moment of worry. Other children struggle through school, attain the occasional A but mostly achieve C and D grades. Some children erratically swing between As and Ds.

If an A-grade child suddenly drops to a D-grade average, his or her behaviour has definitely changed! As long as you can detect this change, then usually you can take some form of action as a parent. (No, I am *not* suggesting that you sell your child!)

If BHP stops performing well, it would be unwise to continue being a shareholder out of a misguided sense of loyalty to the company. Many investors may hold onto their beloved BHP, either through lack of knowledge of the share price, or lack of understanding about the trend. The opportunity cost of holding onto a share that is trending down, while there are others that are trending up, is often very high. Even if you are not losing a great deal of money by sticking with a downtrending share, you are losing the opportunity of getting involved in a profitable share because your capital is tied up. Surely, a more productive strategy would be to re-enter the share when the uptrend is again in place, rather than hold onto a share in a sideways trading range.

As soon as the share swings from being an A-student to a D-student, you can detect this change on the chart using a few simple methods such as trendlines, support/resistance lines and by using some indicators. When a share has stopped behaving in a predictable manner, sell it. With options trading, when the share is behaving positively (by reaching ever-increasing higher peaks), you may be more inclined to write put options. When a share is behaving bearishly and has begun to trend down, you should be more inclined to write call options.

If you know the behavioural characteristics of the shares you are monitoring, you can estimate their likely turning points and trend in the future. I believe that the main way to gain an understanding about a share's behavioural characteristics is to analyse a chart generated by a computer software package. With the help of standardised indicators and your experience in analysing charts, you can estimate the likely future performance of the share. Achieving these skills makes you money in the market. Once you have formed your view on a share, you can then decide which strategy to implement to make money using this information.

Will a software package alone make you money? Probably not... it is just one of the necessary tools of trading the sharemarket. Charting software is now widely available. Despite claims to the contrary, no particular software package will guarantee your success. It is how traders use the tool that makes the difference between consistently winning, or consistently losing.

WHICH INDICATORS SHOULD YOU USE?

Short-term indicators assist in detecting when a short-term uptrend may be reversing. By writing a call option close to this reversal of a short-term uptrend, the premiums on a given option strike price are higher than after the share has fallen further. If the medium-term trend is going down, but the share has a short-term rally, the premiums you will receive on your calls will be higher and your risk will be limited. As you will remember, the closer the share price is to the strike price, the higher the premium. Finding these windows of opportunity for higher option premiums is like stumbling across a gold mine.

When writing put options, I use the indicators to locate the turning point of the short-term downtrend. I maximise my premiums by writing the put as close to a confirmed turning point as possible. If the medium-term trend is going up, but the share experiences a short-term pullback, the premiums you receive on your puts will be high and your risk will be limited.

I always try to trade in the direction of the medium-term *and* short-term trend. I have found that to defy the trend has a damaging effect on my bank balance!

By trading with the trend at all times, you improve your chances of consistently making a profit.

TRENDLINES

Creating trendlines on a chart will assist in answering the following questions:

➲   Is a trend in place?

➲   What is the strength of the trend?

➲   Has the overall trend been broken?

➲   Who is in control, the bulls or the bears?

Using Trendlines to Pinpoint Changes in Direction

➲   For an uptrending share, draw in a trendline below the price points, (see Fig. 5.1).

➲   When price moves below the trendline without reversing upwards again, the uptrend may be broken.

➲   For a downtrending share, draw in a trendline above the price points, (see Fig. 5.2).

➲   When price moves above the trendline without reversing down again, the downtrend may be broken.

➲   The steeper the trend, the more likely it is to be short lived. A steady, longer-term trend is less likely to be broken.

➲   The more price points connected with a straight line, the stronger the trend.

➲   Look for confirmation with other indicators to confirm a trendline break (e.g. the Moving Average Crossover, see page 49) prior to concluding that the trend has reversed.

Fig. 5.1 NATIONAL AUSTRALIA BANK DAILY

Fig. 5.2 BHP WEEKLY

Support and Resistance

The strike price that I choose when writing options is derived through analysis of support and resistance lines. My strike price for out-of-the-money calls and puts is usually positioned at least one to two support/resistance lines away from the current price. This strong resistance/support line that the share has had difficulty penetrating in the past forms a buffer which provides a shelter from the risk, (see Fig. 5.3).

➲ Support and resistance can be seen along a trendline. For the sake of simplicity, however, I will refer to support and resistance lines as running horizontally.

➲ Resistance is where the price is resistant to entering a new, higher price bracket.

➲ Support is where the price is resistant to entering a new, lower price bracket.

➲ Once these lines have been violated, often the price will continue in that direction until it reaches another line of support or resistance. This is often called a breakout, for an upward movement, or breakdown, for a downward movement.

Fig. 5.3 LEND LEASE

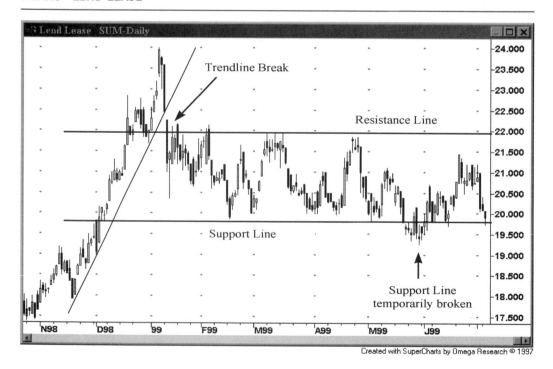

Created with SuperCharts by Omega Research © 1997

◆   These lines may be short term or very well established and long term.

◆   Often lines that were resistance become support and vice versa. This reinforces the significance of that particular line.

Moving Averages

This tool is one of the core indicators utilised by share traders all over the world and moving averages can be found in almost every charting software package available. Moving averages are particularly relevant when trying to locate turning points. By taking the sum of the closing prices and averaging them out, this indicator plots points which, when connected, form a line. This line smoothes out the fluctuations present when looking at the price action on a chart.

Lines that intersect have very important implications. A golden cross is where an indicator, moving average or share price crosses up through a moving average. This is a bullish sign. A dead cross is where an indicator, moving average or share price crosses down through a moving average. This is a bearish sign, (see Fig. 5.4).

Remember to use moving averages of different time frames. This is because moving averages with longer time frames smooth the data to a greater degree than shorter-term moving averages.

Where the price is located, in relation to the moving average, is also important. Prices located above the moving averages are bullish. Prices located below the moving averages are bearish.

Moving averages are not effective if the share is moving sideways. They are most effective if the share is trending up or down.

There are three types of moving averages:

1.   **Simple:** This method of smoothing gives equal weight to each of the data used in the calculation.

2.   **Exponential:** This method of smoothing gives more weight to the most recent data on an exponential basis.

3.   **Weighted:** This is an alternative method of smoothing which gives more weight to the most recent data on a linear basis.

I tend to favour the Exponential Moving Average (EMA). The reason is quite intuitive. Imagine you were interviewing a potential candidate for a corporate position as a Chief Executive Officer in the automotive industry. You flick through the candidate's resume. You notice that 10 years ago, the candidate was a Chief Executive for your major competitor. At this stage, you would begin to feel that this might be the person for the job. However, you then notice that for the last two years he has been working at McDonald's behind the counter. Which piece of information is more important? Probably their most recent job role!

The EMA has the same philosophy as this analogy. It considers the most recent data to carry more weight (on an exponential basis) than the oldest piece of data, (see Fig. 5.4). The Weighted Moving Average (WMA) is also an acceptable tool to use.

Fig. 5.4 NATIONAL AUSTRALIA BANK DAILY

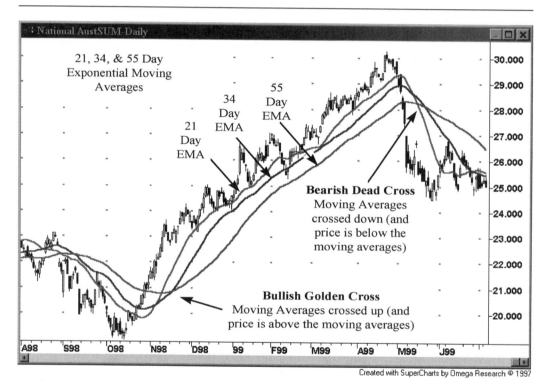

Created with SuperCharts by Omega Research ® 1997

MOMENTUM INDICATORS

Momentum refers to the rate of change of a price trend. Are prices increasing or declining at a faster or slower pace?

The Relative Strength Indicator (RSI), Rate of Change and the Stochastic are all momentum indicators, and there are many more.

In general, overbought and oversold lines represent an intelligent point for anticipating trend reversal (see Fig. 5.5). Overbought lines show that the uptrend may reverse. If the indicator has been trending up and turns down, this is a sell signal. The strength of the sell signal is intensified at historic high points.

Oversold lines show that the downtrend may reverse. If the indicator has been trending down and turns up, this is a buy signal. The strength of the buy signal is intensified at historic low points.

Actual buy and sell signals can come only from a reversal in trend of the actual price, not from a reversal in the momentum. Indices can also be analysed using these indicators to examine whether the industry is likely to change direction in trend.

FIG. 5.5 MOMENTUM INDICATORS

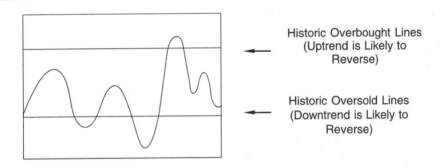

Historic Overbought Lines
(Uptrend is Likely to
Reverse)

Historic Oversold Lines
(Downtrend is Likely to
Reverse)

WHICH TIME FRAMES SHOULD BE USED?

The optimal time frame for each indicator depends on the expiry date that you choose for your option contract. I prefer the medium-term Fibonacci EMAs or momentum time frames of 21, 34 and 55 on a daily and a weekly chart. I use the shorter-term Fibonacci numbers of 5, 8, 13 and 21 on a daily chart to carefully time my entry and exit points.

Fibonacci was a 13th century mathematician and rabbit breeder. (Yes, I am being serious here!) Fibonacci numbers are particularly good at detecting turning points. Therein lies their relevance for traders.

To get you started, here is a list of Fibonacci numbers. If you would like to continue this number progression, you can make further calculations yourself. Each Fibonacci number is the sum of the previous two numbers:

1, 2, 3, 5, 8, 13, 21, 34, 55, 89 .... etc.

Trading Secrets

▶ *Begin with a weekly chart to form an overall view on the entire market, the index and then the share. Draw in trendlines as well as support and resistance lines.*

▶ *Using a daily chart, draw in trendlines as well as support and resistance lines.*

▶ *Use indicators such as moving averages and momentum to establish possible turning points.*

▶ *Use candlestick patterns and short-term indicators to time your entry and exit points (as discussed in the next chapter).*

➔ ➔ ➔ *Candlestick charting is a great tool for technical analysis. The next chapter reveals how candlesticks can make you more money in options trading* ➔ ➔ ➔

Chapter Six

CANDLESTICK

SECRETS

I always suggest that traders take the time to back-test their systems before committing their own money to the market. How would you like to learn about a system that has been back-tested for 300 years? The Japanese have been using candlestick charts since the 17th century and now you can learn the secrets of this amazing method. For more information on this specialist technique refer to my other book *The Secret of Candlestick Charting*.

Drawing a western daily bar chart requires an opening price, a high, a low and a closing price. The vertical line shows the high and low of that period. The two horizontal lines depict the open and close. The open is the horizontal line to the left of the vertical line, and the close is the horizontal line on the right of the vertical line.

Japanese candlesticks utilise the same information as contained in a western bar chart, however they look completely different. The origin of the name is obvious when looking at a chart. A candlestick chart looks like a series of candles with wicks. The thick part of the candle is called the *real body*. This shows the range between the opening and the closing price, (see Fig. 6.1). When the real body is white (or empty), it means that the close was higher than the opening price. When the real body is black (or filled in), the close was lower than the opening price. Some charting packages use the colour green, instead of white, and red, instead of black. I will be discussing the implications of the colour of the candlestick in more detail throughout this chapter.

Fig. 6.1 *DEFINITION OF A CANDLESTICK*

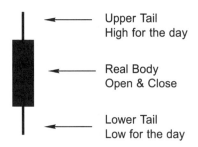

Upper Tail
High for the day

Real Body
Open & Close

Lower Tail
Low for the day

The thin lines above and below the real body are the high and low for that period. These are also essential parts of the candle. These thin lines above and below the real body are called the wicks, tails or the shadows of the candle (regardless of on which side of the real body they are located). I will refer to these lines as tails. The upper tail (the high for the day, on a daily chart) is located above the candlestick's real body, and the lower tail (the low for the day, on a daily chart) is located below the real body. The tails located at both ends of the real body are usually considered to be of less importance than the real body, (as they represent extraneous price fluctuations).

"Amateurs open the market and the professionals close the market."

The open and the close are the most emotionally charged points of the day and therefore they contain particular relevance in the analysis. There is a saying that the amateurs open the market and the professionals close the market. The amateurs in the market have had all night to absorb the rumours and news items about particular shares, and their flurry of activity on the opening of the market reflects this.

The more anxious the trader, the earlier he places his orders with his broker. The closing price is important because the buyers and sellers at this price must live with that decision overnight, so they must be decisive and brave to buy or sell at the final hour. The close of the day is a critical component for many technical analysts in the options and futures markets.

White Candles

The colour of the candle depicts whether the candle is bearish or bullish. When the day closes higher than it opened, this is a positive bullish sign in terms of market sentiment. There is demand for the share and buyers are willing to pay higher and higher prices. They will sacrifice anything just to get their hands on the share. The price is driven up as demand outstrips supply. Greed compels people to purchase the shares and the white colour of the candle clearly shows that the bulls were in control for that period, (see Fig. 6.2).

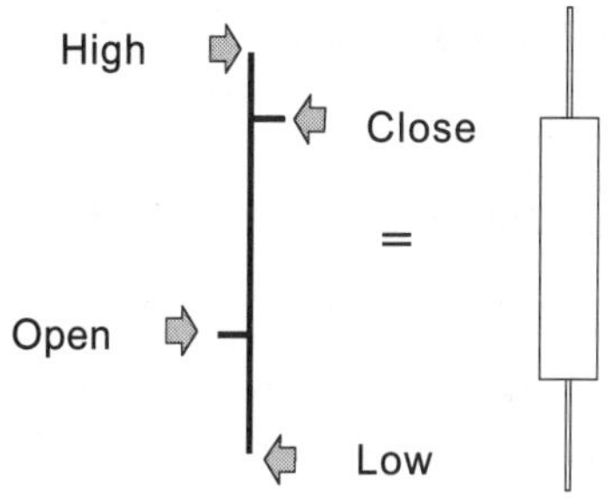

Have you ever heard of the 'Tickle Me Elmo' toy? If you are a parent of young children, it is possible that you have experienced consistent nagging for this highly sought-after collectable item. Tickle Me Elmo is a bright orange soft toy that giggles and vibrates when you tickle it. Just adorable! In the United States especially, the demand for this soft toy was totally underestimated by the manufacturers. Supply was scarce. The price of this popular toy was driven skyward. At the height of this craze, just before Christmas, the asking price for a Tickle Me Elmo was up to $US300! At this exorbitant price, I am sure that parents

FIG. 6.2 THE WHITE CANDLE

High

Close

=

Open

Low

would begin to question whether the toy was a good deal. Demand would probably dwindle. As is evident, when demand is greater than supply, the price will be driven upwards.

BLACK CANDLES

The converse is also true. When the day closes lower than its opening price, it is a sign that sellers are trying to get rid of their shares. This has the effect of driving the share price down. The sellers have fear in their hearts and flood the market with their shares. Hence, the market sentiment is pessimistic creating a far greater supply of shares. Therefore the close is lower than the opening price, and the colour of the candle is black. A black candle clearly shows that the bears were in control for that period, (see Fig. 6.3).

FIG. 6.3 THE BLACK CANDLE

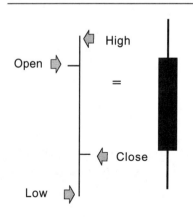

Open

High

=

Close

Low

This tug of war between the bulls and the bears (buyers and sellers) forms the basis for each candlestick and each candlestick pattern formation. A single candlestick, or a group of candles often has particular bullish or bearish significance. Some of these patterns will be discussed later in this chapter.

Whenever gaps or windows (as they are known in candlestick terminology) are present, the strength of the candlestick intensifies. Gaps show that the price activity of the new candlestick is completely above or below the preceding period. Especially when accompanied by significant volume levels, gaps can display a powerful shift in market sentiment. Gaps have a special significance in candlestick philosophy.

WHEN DO YOU USE CANDLESTICKS?

Candlesticks are great at:

➲ Determining short-term trend direction changes

➲ Identifying reversal and continuation patterns.

Continuation patterns suggest that the share will continue over the short term in a particular direction. Reversal patterns mean that a share will change direction completely, or simply flatten into a sideways trend, (see Fig. 6.4).

FIG. 6.4 REVERSAL AND CONTINUATION PATTERNS

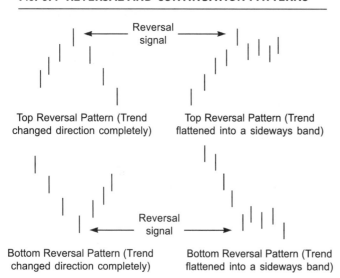

Top Reversal Pattern (Trend changed direction completely)

Top Reversal Pattern (Trend flattened into a sideways band)

Bottom Reversal Pattern (Trend changed direction completely)

Bottom Reversal Pattern (Trend flattened into a sideways band)

The focus of this chapter is the formation and utilisation of candlestick reversal patterns. I have found reversal patterns to be of great benefit in trading options. Reversal patterns are predictive if they occur once the share is trending. If a share is already trading in a sideways band, then reversal patterns will not be effective.

If you do not receive confirmation of the change in trend direction, you would be foolish to act based on the pattern alone. If the candlestick formation is to be trusted and relied upon, await a confirmation of change in the direction of the trend for one or two days before acting!

"If a share is already trading in a sideways band, then reversal patterns will not be effective."

Some patterns have been of particular interest to me when trading options. I shall run through the patterns that have most powerfully assisted my share analysis. For a more comprehensive list of candlesticks, refer to Steve Nison's book called *Japanese Candlestick Charting Techniques*.

I suggest that you use a combination of candlesticks and western techniques. By looking at several indicators, telling the same story, you will have a higher probability of being correct about which way you expect the share to trend. It will take some practice to recognise basic candlestick patterns, but the reward is definitely worth the effort.

COMMON CANDLESTICK PATTERNS

I will begin with some simple reversal candlestick patterns that comprise one candlestick only. I will then progress to two-candle combinations and three-candle combinations. Have a look at the figures to assist your understanding.

The small bars before and after the candlestick formation show the direction of the preceding and following prices on the chart. They have no other special significance in these examples. They are placed on the diagram to assist your understanding of the reversal implications of the candlestick formation.

THE SHOOTING STAR

This pattern displays an upper tail length that is two times the length of the real body, (see Fig. 6.5). There is typically no lower tail in this formation. When there is a gap present between the previous candle and the shooting star, the significance of this formation is intensified. Gaps after the appearance of the shooting star also increase the potency of this signal. This principle is relevant for all candlestick patterns. The star itself can be either white or black. Shooting stars appear at the top of a trend and signify that the bears will be moving in with strength and that a downtrend is likely to occur. When the shooting star hits, run for cover!

FIG. 6.5 THE SHOOTING STAR

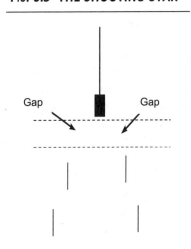

THE DOJI

The doji displays an extremely small real body, (see Fig. 6.6). The open and close are at the same price, or close to the same price, for that period. A doji indicates that the market has temporarily come to an agreement that this particular price represents fair value in the minds of the traders. (After the calm comes the storm!)

Fɪɢ. 6.6 *THE DOJI*

Rickshaw Man Doji   Dragon Fly Doji

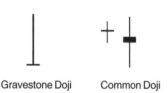

Gravestone Doji   Common Doji

If the share has been uptrending, and a doji appears, the share will often trend downwards. If a share has been trending downwards, and a doji appears, often the share will reverse its downward pattern and begin an uptrend. The share will typically reverse its direction the day after a doji appears in the chart of an uptrending or downtrending stock.

The fewer doji present in the chart, the more significant a signal it is. If there are many doji, the significance of each doji on that chart is markedly diminished.

Although doji will sometimes call the bottom of a trend, they are noted for calling the top of a trend. Remember to always look for confirmation that a doji has actually signalled the reversing of the trend by waiting for a day or two and watching for a change of direction to be evident in the chart.

Spinning Top

Spinning tops are similar to doji, as they both display a small real body, (see Fig. 6.7). The real body on a spinning top formation depicts a larger range from the open to the close than the doji pattern. The tail length is largely unimportant, and the candle can be either white or black. This pattern represents a tug of war between bulls and bears and is accentuated by the presence of a gap before and after its formation.

Fɪɢ. 6.7 *THE SPINNING TOP*

The ultimate tug of war between bulls and bears is represented by a doji, so a spinning top is not quite as strong. This is because the closer the open and the close in a candlestick, the more likely the trend is to reverse in the following few periods. As with all candlestick patterns, remember to watch for confirmation prior to acting on the basis of the candle!

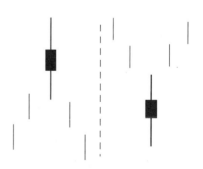

Bearish Spinning Top   Bullish Spinning Top

HAMMERS AND THE HANGING MAN

These patterns display a long tail above or below their real body, (see Fig. 6.8). There is likely to be no tail, or a very short tail on the other side of their real body. The tail length is required to be two times the length of the real body to fulfil the correct definition of this candle. White or black hammers and hanging men have equal significance. Gaps increase the significance of the pattern. Look for these patterns at the top or bottom of trends to signify that a reversal is likely. A hanging man appears at the top of a trend, and hammer/inverted hammer patterns occur at the bottom of a trend.

FIG. 6.8 HAMMERS AND THE HANGING MAN

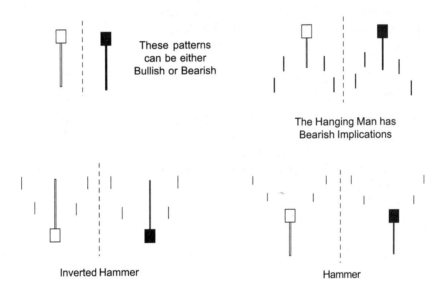

These patterns can be either Bullish or Bearish

The Hanging Man has Bearish Implications

Inverted Hammer

Hammer

The Hammer and Inverted Hammer have Bullish Implications

THE BEARISH ENGULFING PATTERN

This two-candle combination is an extremely effective pattern that often dramatically signifies the end of an uptrend, (see Fig. 6.9). After the appearance of this pattern, prices typically plunge steeply. The second real body of this pattern totally engulfs the first real body and is a bearish sign as the price has closed lower than it opened for that period. The colour of

Fig. 6.9 THE BEARISH ENGULFING PATTERN

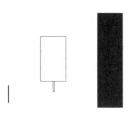

the candles *must* be white for the first candle and black for the second candle. In the eternal tug of war between the bulls and the bears, the bear has arisen victorious and is about to exert its will!

THE BULLISH ENGULFING PATTERN

This particular candle pattern often signifies the end of a downtrend, (see Fig. 6.10). After the pattern has been formed, prices often surge with buyers moving in with enthusiasm. As with its bearish engulfing brother, the second body must totally engulf the body of the first to obtain maximum impact. The colour of the candles *must* be black for the first candle and white for the second candle. Engulfing patterns are very powerful signals.

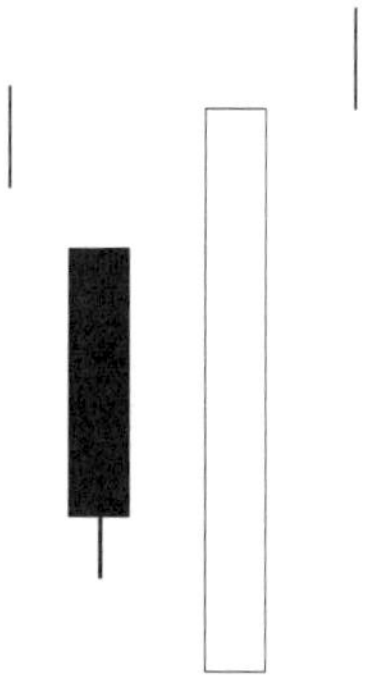

Often shares develop a particular personality which engenders a responsiveness to certain candlestick top and bottom reversal patterns. Many candlestick patterns have equal and opposite reversal patterns which occur at the top and bottom of trends.

Fig. 6.10 THE BULLISH ENGULFING PATTERN

Curiously, when a bearish engulfing pattern has been evident to show us a reverse in the uptrend, a bullish engulfing pattern will often herald the end of the new downtrend.

Fig. 6.11 DARK CLOUD COVER

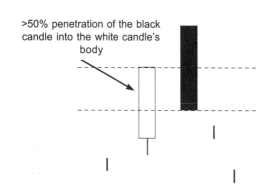

>50% penetration of the black candle into the white candle's body

DARK CLOUD COVER

This two-candle formation is a top reversal pattern, (see Fig. 6.11). It is especially significant if little or no tail exists. The second black candle must penetrate 50% or more into the body of the white candle. The pattern is not quite as significant as the bearish engulfing pattern. In candlestick philosophy, patterns that are more significant display greater penetration levels of one candle into the body of another. In general, the greater the penetration, the more significant the pattern. When there is dark cloud cover, a downpour may be imminent!

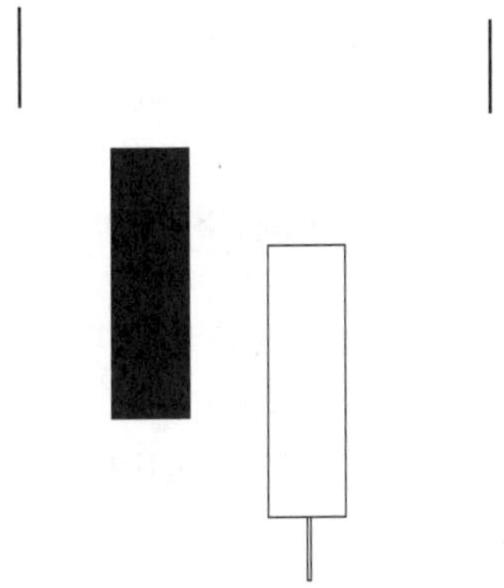

PIERCING PATTERN

This two-candle bottom reversal pattern is the inverse of a dark cloud cover, (see Fig. 6.12). The 50% penetration level of the second candle into the body of the first is equally as important. As with the dark cloud cover, the piercing pattern is not as significant as the bullish engulfing pattern. Engulfing patterns totally cover the body of the initial candle and this characteristic intensifies the likelihood of a reversal.

FIG. 6.12 THE PIERCING PATTERN

EVENING STAR

This bearish three-candle reversal pattern shows a long white real body (1), a small star of either colour (2), then a black real body (3), (see Fig. 6.13). The black candle (3) closes within the body of the white candle (1) or below, preferably after a gap from the star (2). The lower the black candle (3), the more significant the pattern. The evening star pattern is especially potent if there are gaps between each candle. It is a particularly powerful top reversal pattern and it can be observed with surprising regularity.

FIG. 6.13 THE EVENING STAR

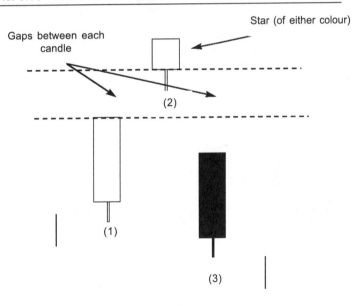

Star (of either colour)

Gaps between each candle

(2)

(1)

(3)

MORNING STAR

This bullish three-candle bottom reversal pattern shows a long black real body (1), a small star of either colour (2), then a white real body (3), (see Fig. 6.14). As with all candlestick patterns, it is especially significant with gaps between each candle.

The white candle (3) closes within the body of the black candle (1) or above, preferably after a gap from the star (2). The higher the white candle (3), the more bullish the pattern.

FIG. 6.14 MORNING STAR

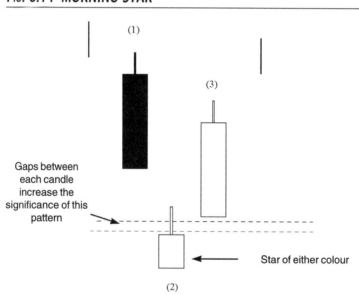

SOME CANDLESTICK EXAMPLES

This chapter provides you with some of the main patterns to get you started in this type of analysis. There are many other types of candlestick formations that can be of assistance in your trading.

Throughout subsequent chapters I will be providing some lucrative examples of options trading using candlesticks for both calls and puts. Once you become accustomed to recognising these patterns, you will begin to see them frequently. Here are some examples of some candlestick patterns that we have reviewed. I have used daily charts to identify these particular patterns, (see Table 6.1).

TABLE 6.1 CANDLESTICK EXAMPLES

Candlestick Pattern	Date and Chart
Hanging Man	TLS 26 Apr 2000
Hammer	CML 22 Sept 2000
Inverted Hammer	FXJ 13 Jul 2000
Spinning Top	AGL 17 Apr 2000
Doji	TLS 17 Aug 2000
Shooting Star	PMP 13 Aug 2000
Bearish Engulfing	CML 12 Oct 2000
Bullish Engulfing	PMP 9 Oct 2000
Evening Star	BHP 11 Jan 2000
Morning Star	BHP 3 Nov 1999
Dark Cloud Cover	CML 29 Aug 2000
Piercing Pattern	AGL 19 Jun 2000

HOW DO CANDLESTICKS ASSIST IN TRADING OPTIONS?

Reversal candlestick patterns can pinpoint changes in short-term direction and assist you in minimising your risk because they give confirmation of a change in trend direction. You can then position your entry point to maximise your cashflow from the premiums you receive, and trade with a higher probability of success.

Imagine that you have detected a downtrending share. You decide that this provides an ideal opportunity to utilise a call writing strategy. As you know, shares go through a series of peaks and troughs, even if their overall direction is downwards. In order to maximise your premiums it is wise to detect these peaks prior to the trend continuing its descent. You could write a call option after a share has peaked and just begun to fall again in value. This will be far more profitable than writing the call when the share is trading at a lower price. Candles can assist in detecting these important turning points.

If you have located an uptrending share, an ideal strategy would be to write an out-of-the-money put. To maximise your put premiums, you can write your puts once the share shows signs of going up in value after recently being in a trough. By locating this turning point, your premiums will be higher due to the share price being closer to your strike price. Candles showing reversal patterns also can provide clues as to when to place your orders.

MAXIMISE YOUR CASHFLOW

When you call your broker with a particular option in mind, he will give you a range of prices that apply to that specific strike price. Your broker may say that the 'spread is between 22¢ and 28¢'. This means that the option which interests you at that strike price is currently trading between 22¢ and 28¢. The first figure in the spread represents the 'bid', (the level at which the buyers would be prepared to buy, e.g. 22¢). The second figure represents the 'ask', (the level at which the sellers would be prepared to sell, e.g. 28¢). If you agree to an amount in the middle of the spread, say 26¢, there is a good chance that your order will be filled. If you hold out for 28¢, you are risking missing out on the deal altogether, unless the share trends causing the premiums to shift in your favour.

The main tool that I use to maximise my premiums is the candlestick. The trick to increasing premiums is to write out-of-the-money call options on days when the market is at a short-term high, and out-of-the-money put options on days when the market is at a short-term low. Candlesticks will provide guidance on these turning points allowing you to time your trades with precision.

Many candles will provide a clear indication as to the likely progression of the share price for the following day.

If you have a clear indication that the share you are watching will go *up* in value throughout the day, you could write calls late in the day and position your order at the top end of the spread. Alternatively, you could write puts early in the day and position your order at the bottom end of the spread.

If you have a clear indication that the share you are watching will go *down* in value throughout the day, you could write calls early in the day and position your order at the bottom end of the spread. Alternatively, you could write puts late in the day and position your order at the top end of the spread. These methods will assist in maximising the premiums that you will receive when placing your orders.

For example, after an evening star formation, a series of black candles often forms. This shows that the bears have begun to thrash the bulls. Using this information, have a think about how you could obtain a superior call option premium.

A logical way to benefit from the series of black candles is to place your call option order in the morning while the share price is high. Based on your knowledge, you can estimate that the share price will fall away during the day, therefore the call option premiums will dwindle. By placing your order in the morning, you have a good chance of receiving the maximum call option premium available on that day.

Even if the candlestick pattern is not exactly perfect, of more importance is the fact that the pattern can give you an indication of the direction in which the share might trend. Some patterns come close to the definition for an evening star, but there may not be gaps between each day for example. This does not matter as long as the effect is the same. If you think the candlestick formation resembles a shooting star, it is best to wait for confirmation for one to two days before acting. This confirmation step is often skipped by candlestick traders and leads to poor trading results.

It is possible to trade options without the use of candlesticks. Many of the trades I make are not based on an ideal candlestick formation. However, the trades that _are_ made based on a candlestick pattern have made me a higher level of profit and have been made with a higher level of certainty than if the candlestick pattern was not present.

Trading Secrets

▶ **By combining candlesticks with other technical charting methods you will maximise the premiums per option trade and make trades with a higher probability of success.**

▶ **Reversal patterns mean that a share will change direction completely, or simply flatten into a sideways trend. These patterns are ideal for use when trading choppy shares.**

Over the years I have implemented every call and put option strategy that you will see in the next two chapters. I will provide examples wherever possible in order to illustrate key points. The ideal candlestick patterns that are reliable for trading options do not occur in the share chart every month. However, when these patterns do occur, the trading opportunities that they present are great. Wherever I provide an example of a candlestick trade that conformed to the candlestick patterns discussed, I have called it a 'candlestick classic'.

Trading Secrets

▶ *Always wait for a day or two for confirmation prior to acting on a candlestick pattern.*

▶ *Candlesticks are most effectively used for short-term trades, or to time an entry point into trades of any duration. Patterns are evident on both daily and weekly charts. However, if you wait for confirmation from a weekly chart the short-term trade may have altered.*

REVIEW

1)   Now it is your turn. Have a look at the charts on pages 67 and 68 and try your hand at identifying some of the patterns that have been discussed in this chapter.

ANSWERS

1)   See Fig. 6.17 and Fig. 6.18. Although I have indicated the main formations, you may have found extra candlestick patterns on these charts. Well done! Keep practising and you will get the hang of it.

➔   ➔   ➔   *We are now ready to put all of this information together and have a look at some call writing strategies...*   ➔   ➔   ➔

FIG. 6.15 BHP DAILY

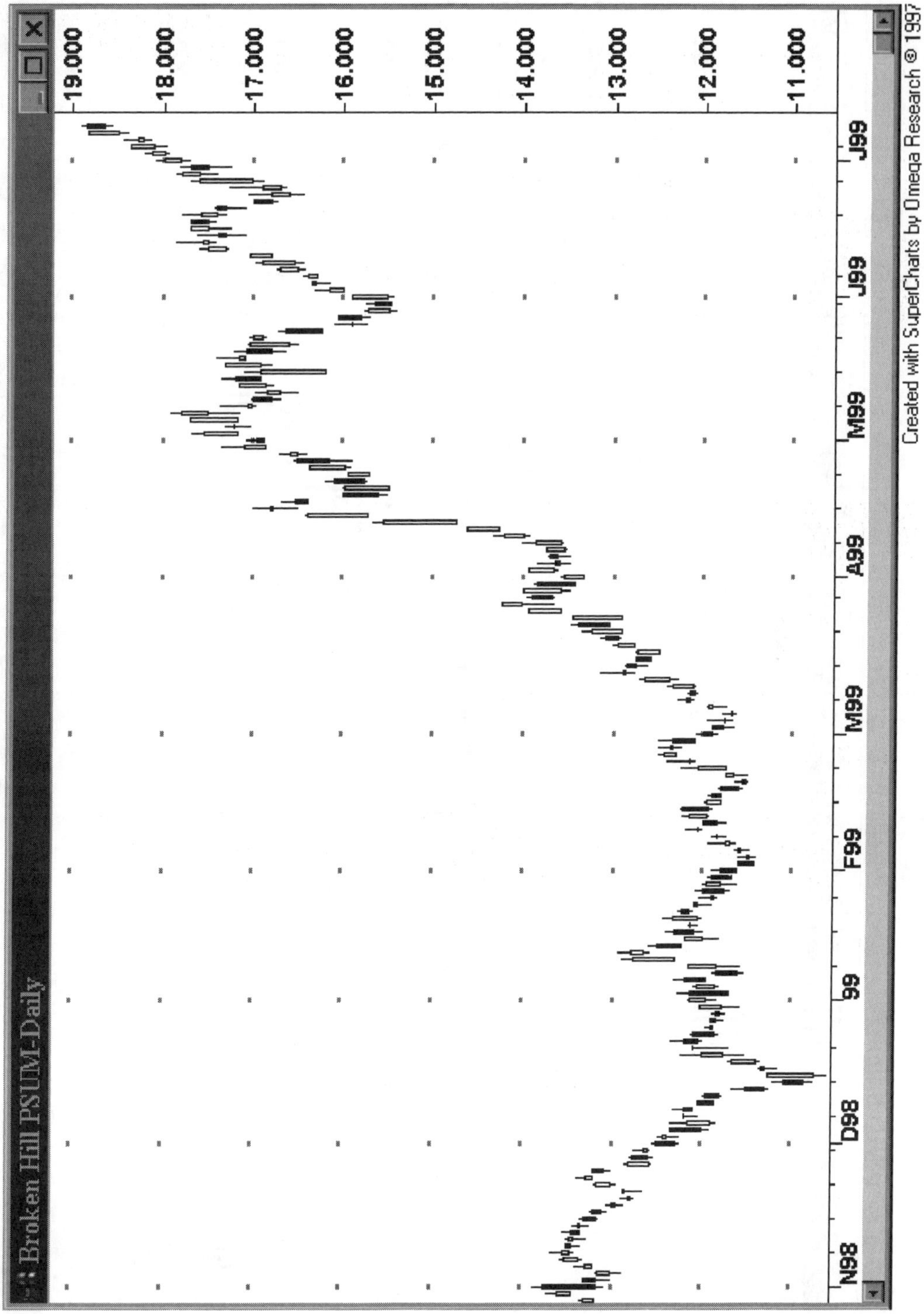

Broken Hill PSUM-Daily

Created with SuperCharts by Omega Research © 1997

FIG. 6.16 OPTUS DAILY

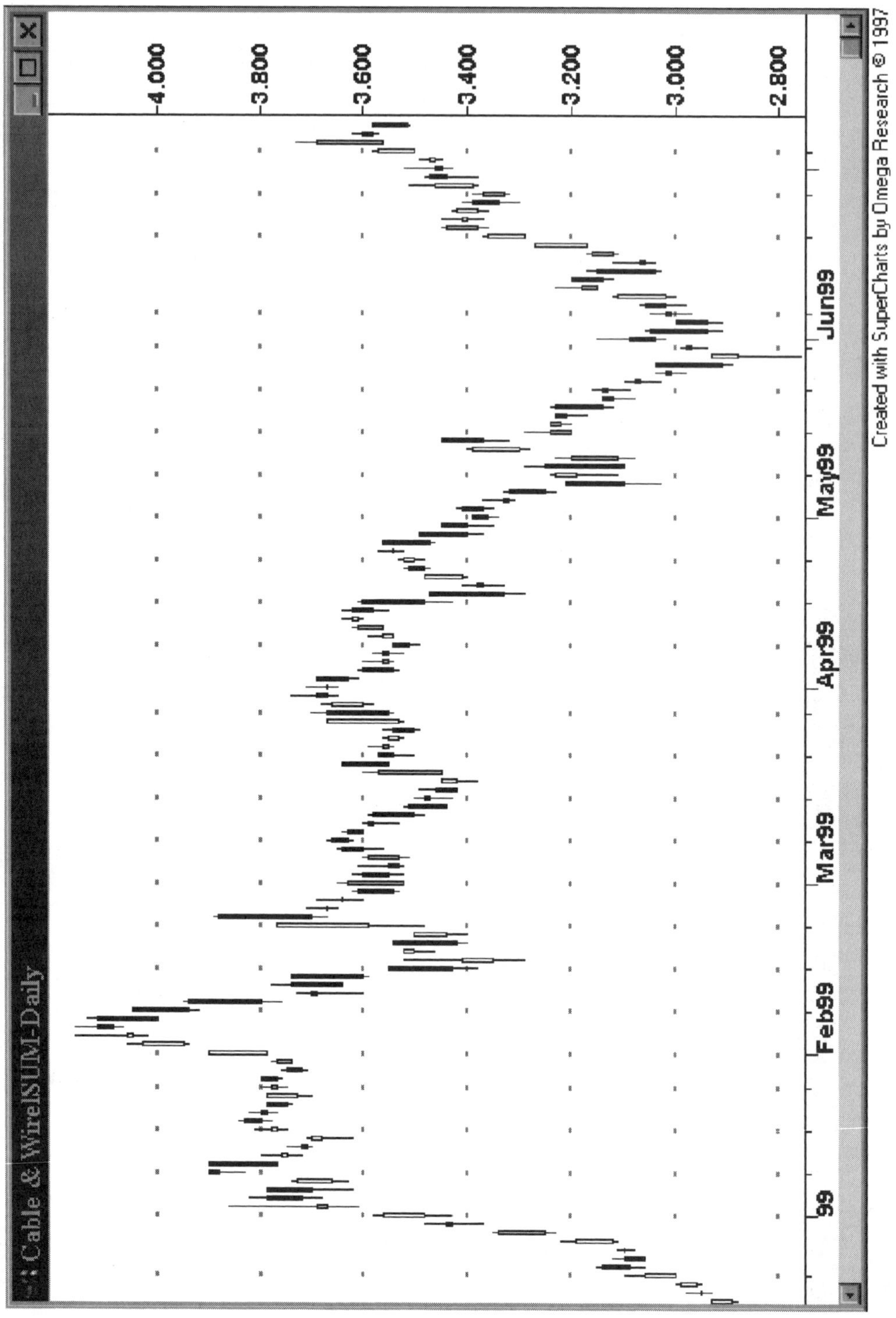

Fig. 6.17 BHP DAILY

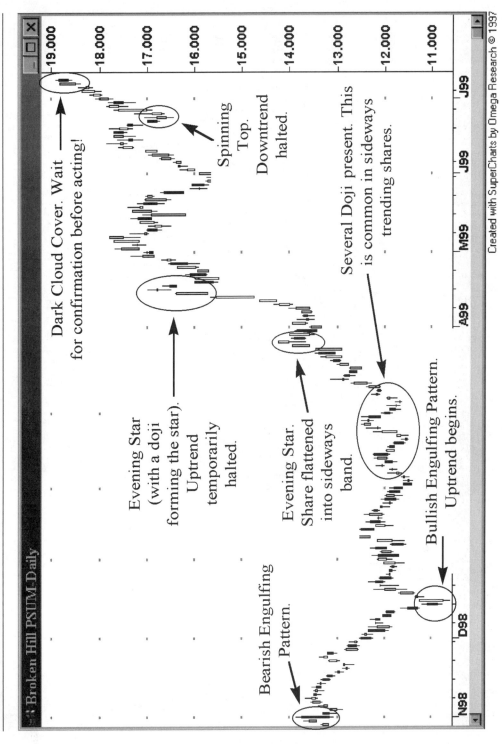

Broken Hill PSUM-Daily

Dark Cloud Cover. Wait for confirmation before acting!

Evening Star (with a doji forming the star). Uptrend temporarily halted.

Evening Star. Share flattened into sideways band.

Bearish Engulfing Pattern.

Bullish Engulfing Pattern. Uptrend begins.

Several Doji present. This is common in sideways trending shares.

Spinning Top.

Downtrend halted.

Created with SuperCharts by Omega Research © 1997

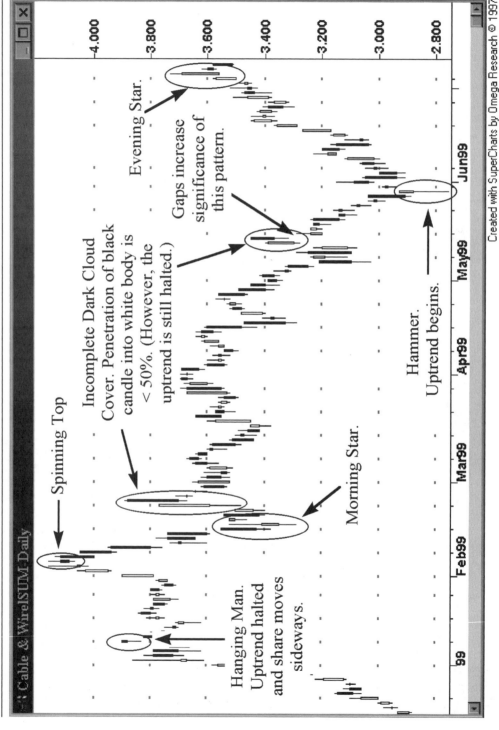

FIG. 6.18 OPTUS DAILY

Chapter Seven

CALL WRITING

STRATEGIES

H ere is a way that you can make more profit if you already own shares...

THE BUY AND WRITE STRATEGY

If you are a beginner to the options market, the buy and write is the safest and simplest strategy to implement if you already own shares.

This method is where you write covered calls over shares that you already own. To implement this strategy, you must own or purchase shares that can be used as the underlying security. If you are not certain as to whether your shares are suitable for this strategy, refer to *The Australian* or *The Australian Financial Review* newspapers, which list options activity. In addition, if you own less than 2000 shares in the underlying security, it may not be worth your while writing calls, as your options profit may be negligible after brokerage.

"The buy and write is the safest and simplest strategy to implement."

If you are exercised and the strike price is above the price you paid for the share initially, you will achieve a capital gain as well as keep the premium. By writing these covered calls, you are making your portfolio work hard! Writing a call will bring in some regular income in addition to waiting for the share to pay out a dividend. Many traders have found that by implementing this strategy, their returns have safely increased, and that the additional cashflow has been a welcome change from waiting for dividend payments. If you would like to make your portfolio return an extra 5% to 15% a year, this may be the strategy for you.

The key to this strategy is to write a call at the level that you would be happy to sell the share. Imagine you owned BHP shares. If the price went up $1 within a short period, you may be very comfortable taking some profits from BHP. If this is the case, then write an out-of-the-money call at a strike price that is $1 away from the current share price. If you end up selling BHP, you are happy because you have realised a capital gain on the share. If you do not sell your share, then you get to keep the premium that you have received as a result of writing the call. Either way, you will be satisfied with the result.

As a guide, I suggest that you write call options with a one- to three-month expiry date for a minimum of 5¢ per share in premium to be attained per month. For example, a three-month expiry contract would need to generate at least 15¢ per share in premium. By writing a call with a short period of time to go before expiry, you are minimising the chance that the share will uptrend strongly without warning.

Longer dated calls will bring you greater premiums, but the odds are against you in terms of being able to predict the ultimate share price at the end of the option contract. If the share trends up strongly and you have written longer dated contracts, you may ultimately sell your share for a price that is far lower than the available share price at the time of expiry.

Although this method works very well, a few words of caution are required:

a)   If the share you buy or own goes down in value, you will experience a capital loss. It is NEVER wise to purchase a downtrending share! When purchasing a share for the first time, take care to purchase shares with a high probability of trending up. However, if you own a share which is in a flat trading band, or slight short-term downtrend, the income made on the premiums when you write calls will help to offset the opportunity cost that you may incur, and will certainly make you feel better in the process. The buy and write strategy is especially relevant if you are utilising margin lending. By writing calls, you will be positively influencing your cashflow in order to assist in covering your margin lending interest payment requirements.

b)   The call option, when exercised, may prevent you from deriving greater profits from your share, should the uptrend continue. If you can be happy with the amount of profit that you will receive from the share if exercised, then you are probably a candidate for this strategy. There is nothing worse than looking back in time and seeing that you sold your share just before a major bull run occurred! To perform a buy and write strategy well, you need to have the attitude that you are happy to sell the share at the strike price of the option.

c) You must be willing to sell your share in order to use this strategy, or you will need to take some hefty defensive action to remove yourself from the options contract. If you are emotionally hanging onto the shares that you own, being forced to sell them may be a gut-wrenching experience. Although it is not wise to have 'favourite' shares, it is often more difficult to have an impartial attitude towards a share that has made you a lot of money in the past.

d) The Options Clearing House (OCH) can use your shares as security (as well as cash in your cash management account) to cover option margin requirements. Therefore, you may be required to sell shares to cover the options that you have written or been exercised on. Watch your exposure levels and make sure that you have enough equity in shares or cash prior to writing any options contract.

An Example

When Telstra 1 floated I purchased a parcel of shares and happily watched the share price increase in value. By writing out-of-the-money calls at least two or three strike prices away from the price of Telstra on a monthly basis, I was able to generate an income from this share. Each month that Telstra went up in value I made a capital gain on paper, (see Fig. 7.1). However, because I was writing calls, I was also picking up a few hundred dollars each month from the premiums. On a monthly basis, this premium money was dropping directly into my bank account. Rather than awaiting a dividend to assist my cashflow situation, I was earning additional cash from my call writing activities. Writing calls was particularly useful when Telstra was trading in a sideways band, as although I was not making money on the share, I was making money from the premiums I was collecting. Figure 7.1 shows some of the written call option positions that I maintained over Telstra and when I was finally exercised in January. Often a sudden sharp share price rally will increase the probability of being exercised. When I was finally exercised on my written calls, I was happy with the sale price that I received for Telstra, as well as the premiums I had made on a monthly basis from my written calls.

If you own shares that are uptrending, writing covered options maximises your cashflow. (Usually when writing *naked* call options you will need to locate a sideways or downtrending share.)

FIG. 7.1 TELSTRA DAILY

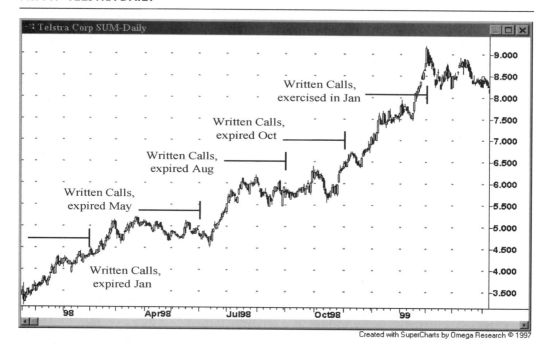

Written Calls, exercised in Jan

Written Calls, expired Oct

Written Calls, expired Aug

Written Calls, expired May

Written Calls, expired Jan

Created with SuperCharts by Omega Research © 1997

Trading Secrets

▸ **The buy and write strategy is the safest and simplest to implement if you already own shares.**

▸ **The key to this strategy is to write a call at a level that you would be happy to sell the share.**

▸ **Write a call option with a one- to three-month expiry for a minimum of 5¢ premium per share to be attained per month.**

NAKED CALL WRITING

This strategy is most appropriate if your view of the market is bearish, or if you believe that the share is moving sideways.

As you will remember from Chapter 2, naked calls are written when you do not own the underlying security. By now you should realise that if you are exercised on a call option, you must deliver shares at the strike price level to the option buyer. If you do not own the shares in a naked call situation, then you must buy the shares at the market price, in order to deliver them at the stipulated strike price.

If you have detected a share trending down, you can write an out-of-the-money call that is at least one, or preferably two, support/resistance levels away from the share price. This is a very conservative strategy because markets rarely spike up suddenly.

Shares generally increase in value slowly, but sharply drop in value. The concept is similar to pushing a boulder up a hill. Although it takes a lot of effort to get the boulder up the hill, it is very easy for the boulder to roll quickly down the slope (possibly bowling you over in the process).

More aggressive traders could write an in- or at-the-money call on a share that they believe will steeply downtrend. When you are starting out, I suggest that you stick with a conservative strategy. Begin by writing out-of-the-money calls. This will maximise your chances of success and give you an opportunity to learn about the options market without an inordinate amount of risk.

Usually I write naked out-of-the-money calls over a downtrending or sideways moving stock. However, an alternative is to write a call over the top of an uptrending stock that seems to have run out of puff. Your momentum indicators may provide useful assistance in analysing shares to detect when the uptrend is likely to reverse. Candlesticks are also very useful when using this strategy.

Obviously this method has greater levels of risk than choosing a downtrending share and writing a call. However, if you believe you have detected a turning point, writing calls over such a share can be extremely profitable. This is a viable strategy, especially if you write your option above one or two significant support/resistance lines away from the current stock price.

If you are keen to try out this strategy of writing a call over an uptrending stock that has run out of momentum, it may be wise to have a think about the psychology of people who buy shares. Usually buyers of choppy or volatile shares do not like to purchase the share at an all-time high. This gives them an uncomfortable feeling, as the share has never before been at this price, and there is very little to confirm whether it will continue to achieve greater heights in the future.

Regular, consistent uptrending shares bring a lot of comfort to potential share purchasers. If the share is strongly uptrending into blue sky already, sharebuyers are more likely to experience greed and continue the sharebuying frenzy. A share that is continually reaching all-time highs means that traders have not yet experienced a loss when trading that share. For this reason, sentiment is positive and it is very difficult to pinpoint a reversal of this continuous upward thrust. Caution needs to be applied if you intend to write calls over shares trending into blue sky territory.

Trading Secrets

▸ *Avoid a call writing strategy if you have a share that is trading at an all-time high. It is very difficult to detect a turning point when looking at a share that consistently trades at higher and higher prices!*

▸ *It is wise to choose a choppy share that has experienced solid resistance at a particular level. By looking for confirmation of a turning point and writing your calls above one or two established resistance levels, you are maximising your chances of not being exercised.*

AN AMP EXAMPLE

AMP's downtrend had become quite established from December 1998 to February 1999, (see Fig. 7.2). Perfect territory to write a series of calls over several months! This generated a healthy fund injection into my cash management account. On 3 February 1999, the price of AMP was $19.50, so I wrote a $21.50 AMP call and attained 8¢ in premium for a 25 February 1999 expiry. AMP closed at $18.92, well below $21.50. On 4 March 1999, I wrote another call at the $20.00 level and attained an 18¢ premium for a 25 March 1999 expiry. AMP closed at $17.55, again below the $20.00 level. I continued this strategy for several months. I have also shown my April and May trades in Fig. 7.2. It is possible to make money on a downtrending share with the correct strategy!

By repeating this call writing strategy on a month-to-month basis on a downtrending share, a substantial amount of money can be made. By writing options with a shorter-term expiry date such as described above, I am lessening my chances of a share rebounding or trending upwards strongly and threatening my open positions. This is an example of finding a downtrending share and then consistently writing calls over the share for the duration of the downtrend.

Fig. 7.2 AMP DAILY

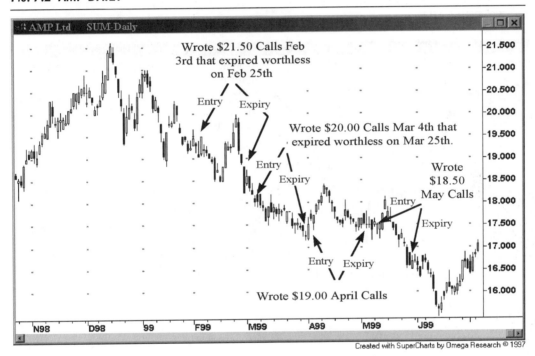

Created with SuperCharts by Omega Research © 1997

A BHP Candlestick Classic

BHP was in a long-term downtrend beginning in July 1997, which represented an opportunity to write call options. A candlestick bearish engulfing pattern was recognised on the 16/17 July 1998, (see Fig. 7.3). This represented an extremely good opportunity to maximise my premiums and to confirm my view about a temporary peak in the continuing downtrend. After the pattern appeared, I waited two days for confirmation. I wanted to make sure that the pattern was going to fulfil my expectation, and that BHP's share price was, in fact, going to go down in value. In addition to the candlestick pattern, I noted that the short-term uptrend trendline of BHP had just been broken, and the five and eight day EMA had crossed down. These three indications added undeniable confirmation of my theory that BHP was going down. On 22 July 1998, I wrote call options with a $15.00 strike price, and proceeded to monitor my positions over the course of the month. On the expiry day (30 July 1998), BHP closed at $13.61. My written calls were well and truly safe and I pocketed a lovely profit for the trade. This is an example of using candlestick formations to maximise the call option premiums that you can receive from the market.

Fig. 7.3 BHP DAILY

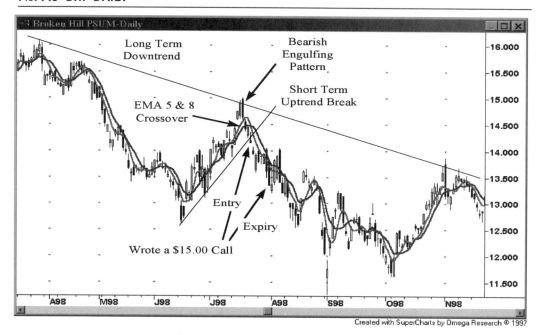

Created with SuperCharts by Omega Research ® 1997

AN NCP CANDLESTICK CLASSIC

NCP had shot up in value at a very steep angle from mid-June 1998, (see Fig. 7.4). Keeping in mind that what goes up quickly often has trouble continuing to defy gravity, I took a close look at my candlestick chart. To my delight, on the 30 June 1998, there was a magnificent spinning top with the idyllic gap formation before and after this candle. After waiting a couple of days for confirmation, it became evident that the share price was beginning to flatten out. I wrote a call option with a $14.00 strike price on 7 July 1998. The expiry day was 30 July 1998 and the share closed at $12.05. The spinning top had actually signified the beginning of a new downtrend. This is an example of writing a call over the top of an uptrending stock that seems to have 'run out of puff'. What a terrific way to pocket some extra income!

Fɪɢ. 7.4 NEWS CORPORATION DAILY

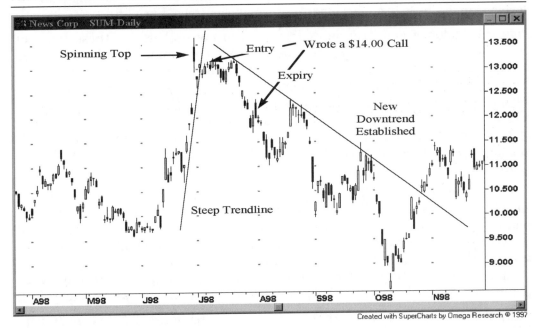

Created with SuperCharts by Omega Research ® 1997

Trading Secrets

▸ *Implement a basic call writing strategy if your view is bearish or if you believe that the share is trending sideways.*

▸ *Write out-of-the-money calls at a strike price that is at least one or two support/resistance levels away from the share price.*

▸ *Unless there is some sign of a reversal, avoid a call writing strategy if you have a share that is trading at an all-time high. Choose a choppy share that has experienced solid resistance at a particular level.*

WRITING OUT-OF-THE-MONEY CALLS ON INDICES

It is possible to write call options over some indices. The index that I tend to focus on with call option writing is the UK FTSE (or FT-100). The FTSE is the London stock market index. Taking advantage of heightened volatility often available in index trades means that attractive premiums can be derived on a short-term or medium-term basis, (see Fig. 7.5).

Peter G. Moloney and Associates Pty Ltd are my brokers for these types of trades. Dealing with Moloney's provides an added advantage for the newcomer to the option market. Moloney's calculates the strike price based on the volatility of the index for their clients, and this takes the guesswork out of which strike price to choose. In addition, because the FTSE is an international index, Moloney's has all of the necessary contacts required to set up a deal of this complexity. If I attempted to perform a trade like this by myself, it is possible that I would have to source a broker in England ... a cumbersome procedure.

Usually, shares 'go up by the staircase and then drop down the elevator shaft', so to speak. In other words, they creep upwards in price slowly, yet plunge in price dramatically. This means that it would be foolhardy indeed to write put options on indices which will drop sharply and often without warning in a market correction! Beware of any broker who suggests this strategy of put writing under indices (without suggesting ways to limit your potential loss, such as with the purchase of a put at a lower strike price).

Statistically, history reveals that crashes or corrections of between 10% to 50% have occurred within days or weeks. This does not provide a lot of warning to jump out of a written put!

Because an index represents a large number of shares it includes shares trending up and down, and the risk of an extremely sharp sustained uptrend is minimised. Writing calls over the FTSE has been extremely profitable for many option traders.

With shorter-term options, there is less probability they will become in-the-money when compared to longer-term options. Statistically, there is a lower probability that a deep out-of-the-money call option will become in-the-money in comparison with one of a longer-time frame. For this reason, when dealing with an index option I usually keep the term to less than eight weeks, as well as writing out-of-the-money option strike prices. The ideal strike price is positioned above the recent levels of volatility and above a strong support/resistance line, plus a zone for error. In other words, historically the index has shown that it will only go up by a certain amount within any one period. I prefer that the position of my strike price takes this into account.

Be aware that the expiry date for options trades over indices may differ from the expiry dates for other Australian based options. Check this prior to conducting any trades using this method.

A FTSE EXAMPLE

The FTSE was in uptrend for most of the trades that I have conducted using written calls. However, the volatility of this index allows for quite substantial out-of-the-money premiums. For this reason, I could position my strike price far enough away from the actual value of the FTSE to remove myself from unacceptable levels of risk.

The beginning of a sideways movement in the FTSE allowed me to write a call on 27 May 1999 at a 6700 strike. On 27 May, the FTSE closed at 6199. For this transaction I received 13 points per contract, which is the approximate equivalent of $A265 per contract. The closing level of the FTSE on 18 June 1999 was 6493. For each contract written, a deposit of $5000 is required. By writing a call above the average volatility level for the previous month and above a significant resistance line, I stacked the odds of having a winning trade in my favour.

FIG. 7.5 FTSE 100 - DAILY

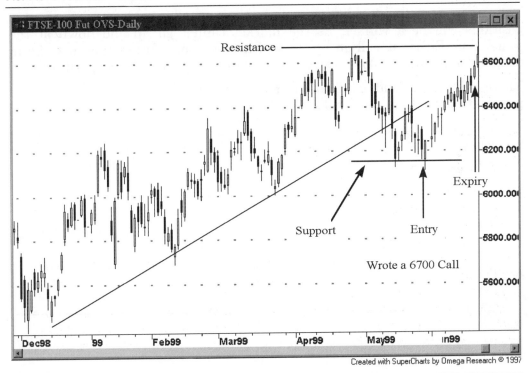

Trading Secrets

▸ **Use the services of an experienced broker to write call options over international indices.**

▸ **Never write uncovered put options on indices due to the risk of a sharemarket correction. (A covered put is where you have purchased a put at a strike price lower than your written put).**

THE STRANGLE

Option writing is one of the few strategies that thrives if a share is trending sideways, so why not double your chances of making money by writing both calls and puts. At any stage, there are many shares trading sideways, instead of trending up or down. With a strangle strategy, instead of experiencing frustration at sideways movement, you can profit from it!

With a strangle strategy, I write puts below *and* write calls above the current share price.

The great part about this strategy is that usually, at least one of your positions will be a winner, as the market cannot go up and down at the same time. Either it will go up, in which case your written calls may be in danger, or it will go down, and your written puts may be jeopardised.

There are ex-dividend implications that can affect this strategy. For more information on this, have a look at Chapter 10, The Dividend Effect.

As a suggestion, it is wise to write calls and puts using this method along previously strong support/resistance lines. This lessens your chance of the share breaking through these lines. This is an extremely effective strategy.

Trading Secrets

Write out-of-the-money calls and puts on shares that are trending sideways.

REVIEW

1) If you own shares, how can you derive higher levels of return using option strategies?

2) Should you write calls if your view is that the share will skyrocket upwards in price?

3) If a share is trending in a defined sideways band, what options strategy can you implement?

4) When writing options on international indices, should you write uncovered puts?

ANSWERS

1) Utilising a buy and write strategy will allow you to experience capital growth on your shares in addition to the premium that is received by writing out-of-the-money call options.

2) No. Definitely avoid writing calls if you believe that the share will go up in value dramatically.

3) If a share is moving sideways, write both calls and puts that are out-of-the-money. This is called a strangle strategy.

4) No. Write *calls* over indices or cover your written puts by buying a put at a lower strike price. Writing calls over indices is a conservative strategy. If you write an uncovered put on an index, your losses could be catastrophic if a significant decrease in the value of the index occurs.

➜ ➜ ➜ *Put writing is next on the agenda. Keep reading to discover some specific strategies that will help you to make money using put options...* ➜ ➜ ➜

Chapter Eight

PUT WRITING

STRATEGIES

TRADING WITHIN YOUR LIMITS

A n essential concept when writing puts is to understand that you must trade within your limits. As a put option writer, your exposure level is the total possible amount of money that you would be liable for if the options were exercised. This is a more critical concept when writing put options, rather than calls. If a significant fall occurs there is a high probability that the majority of your written puts will be at risk. Your risk when writing options is technically unlimited. If the share price drops from $30 to $5, the effect could be devastating if you cannot financially cover the contracts you have written.

Having written puts underneath a falling share is a terrifying situation. The whole world is coming down on top of you and you either need to get out of the way or risk grievous financial injury.

It is highly recommended that at all times, the level of put option exposure is not more than the level of cash reserves available if the option were to be exercised. For example, if you were to write five NCP puts at $12.50 strike, your put option exposure would be $62,500.

The following calculation may shed some light on this:

Five NCP contracts at 1000 shares per contract = 5000 shares

5000 shares x $12.50 strike price = $62,500

Therefore, the put option exposure for this transaction is $62,500.

If you prefer to maintain a smaller level of cash in reserve and you own an equivalent amount of capital in shares, you must be prepared to sell your stock holdings or to utilise margin lending. The total asset combination of your cash, stock holdings and margin lending must cover your written put exposure.

When I was first learning about options, I did not understand the significance of trading within my limits. The importance of exposure on written put levels had completely escaped me as a concept. In about the third month of learning about options, I decided that it was time to start really trading. After opening many written put positions, I added up the money I had made and decided that I deserved a reward for my clever analysis. I drove with haste up to the shops and proceeded to spend my hard-earned cash...

Just as I was handing over the Visa for my last purchase, an aggravating little voice started ringing in my ears. "What if the market crashes?" it said. After a quick mental calculation I realised that I had written $800,000 in puts greater than I could cover if the market crashed! Horror, Horror!

The trip back from the shops was a hurried blur of panic as I rushed home to phone my broker. Under my direction, he closed out most of my open written positions. I minimised my exposure and I have never gone over my limits again. It is just not worth it.

It is your responsibility, not your broker's, to monitor your exposure levels! Some brokers will let you keep writing puts endlessly, regardless of the risk involved. They are happy to keep collecting their brokerage fees with no concern for your welfare if the market takes a sudden downturn. If you are going to play the options game, it is wise to play by the rules and keep track of your own trading.

"It is your responsibility, not your broker's, to monitor your exposure levels!"

Other brokers are particularly resistant to writing uncovered options. This may be due to either a lack of experience in options, or an acknowledgement of the risks in writing uncovered positions. You may have to interview a few different brokers to ensure that they are willing to fulfil the strategies that you require. Be prepared to ask as many questions as possible to ensure that you have found a broker to match your requirements.

WAYS TO LIMIT YOUR RISK

If the market turns against you it will be without warning, so why place yourself in a position where you could end up with a large financial burden. In reference to your written puts, a fall will threaten your positions, and it may be difficult to take timely defensive actions. Here is a method where you can cover your written puts and diminish the risk associated with option trading. I have already alluded to this method in the discussion of writing puts under international indices (see Chapter 7).

You could choose to limit your amount of risk by writing a put at a particular strike price and then buying a put at a lower strike price. This effectively creates a covered written put. Because the bought put is further away from the share price, and therefore further away from the risk, it will cost less than the premium that you have received from your written put. This method will cap the loss level at a reasonable rate. This takes the fear out of writing puts and can free up your exposure levels.

The level of call option exposure is less stringent than put option exposure as the market tends to drop in value more quickly than it peaks. The main concern with written calls is if a take-over is announced above your strike price on the physical stock, or if another fundamental reason causes the stock price to increase dramatically. If you have covered calls where you own the underlying stock, then a sharp uptrend should not be of concern to you.

The risk lies in naked call positions, as you are required to deliver the shares at the strike price level if exercised. With naked calls, you need to purchase the share on the open market for delivery to the exerciser of the call. For example, you may be required to purchase the share at the current price of $20.00. Because of your call option, you may be required to deliver this share at $15.00 (i.e. the strike price of the option contract). This represents a significant loss. There are, however, a few ways that you can protect yourself. You can either take a defensive action, or you can implement a call buying strategy.

To protect yourself from risk in this situation, you could buy a call at a strike price greater than your written call strike price. The call premium at the higher strike price would be considerably less than the written call strike. This would have the effect of capping your potential loss on your written calls.

As you have probably guessed, these methods of buying puts and calls to limit loss will also limit the premium received in total. You need to consider your comfort zone, and whether you are happy having uncovered option positions. It may take you a while to fully come to grips with the implications of this discussion. By gaining an understanding of how to trade within your limits you will consistently achieve good returns in the options market. Option trading without an understanding of these concepts will have a rollercoaster effect on your finances. Sometimes you will make incredible gains, but occasionally you will make a trade that will wipe out more than any previous gains that you have made. Some option traders have managed to lose their homes as they were not prompt at taking defensive actions!

The other form of risk inherent in trading options is if a broker places a trade in error on your behalf. This is a surprisingly common phenomenon if you are not using a broker experienced in this field. If your phone calls are not recorded by your broker, perhaps consider faxing or emailing confirmation of your orders. This will assist in proof of indemnity in case the broker misunderstands your intentions, or if an error is made when placing the order.

Trading Secrets

To limit your risk in writing options, buy the same number of contracts one strike price further out-of the-money.

Here are some lucrative put writing strategies.

BASIC PUT WRITING

If you have detected an uptrending share, you could write an out-of-the-money put at a price that you believe the share will not penetrate.

For the more aggressive traders, you could write an in- or at-the-money put on a share that you believe will steeply uptrend. Beginners in the options market should avoid aggressive strategies such as this. Serve your apprenticeship by learning about conservative strategies. When you have developed the skills and experience to deal with heightened levels of risk, then you can graduate to in- or at-the-money strategies.

When you are starting to write options, it is wise to write a put under a share that you would not mind owning. If you feel that the purchase of a share would be appropriate at $9.00, and you would be prepared to pay that amount, you could write a $9.00 put. If you were exercised, you would end up buying the share for $9.00. If you are not exercised due to the share uptrending, then you will get to keep the premium. Either way, you will be happy with the transaction.

Another strategy is to write a put under a downtrending stock that seems to have run out of downward momentum. This is also a viable strategy if you write your option below one or two significant support/resistance lines away from the current share price. You must feel confident that you have chosen a share that has reached a turning point and will reverse its downtrend, and either trade in a flat lateral band, or upwards in direction. Momentum indicators and candlesticks are essential tools to assess which share is displaying these characteristics.

Remember the concepts that were discussed in the previous chapter, regarding the strength of a trend in an uptrending stock? We decided that it was important not to write a call over a stock that was trading at an all-time high. Similar lessons hold true when looking at a downtrending share. If the share has built up considerable momentum in its downtrend, it will be difficult to locate an exact turning point. The longer the share has been trending down, the more difficult it will be to stop this downtrend. Writing a put option underneath a share with significant downward momentum is a dangerous practice.

A more prudent strategy would be to write a put option under a share that is trending upwards, or sideways. Have a look at the following LLC example in Fig. 8.1. This is an example of writing a put under a share that is trading in a sideways band.

Trading Secrets

▸ *Write an out-of-the-money put that is at least one or two support/resistance levels away from the share price. This strategy is most appropriate if your view of the share is bullish or that it is likely to move sideways.*

▸ *For the more aggressive traders, you could write an in- or at-the-money put on a share that you believe will steeply uptrend.*

▸ *Another alternative is to write a put under a downtrending stock that seems to have run out of downward momentum.*

An LLC Trade

An example of a basic put writing strategy is an LLC trade that I performed in May 1999, (see Fig. 8.1). With six weeks to go before expiry, LLC was trading in a flat channel between $19.90 and $22.00. At the time that I performed the transaction I believed that there was a chance that LLC would break upwards. (Otherwise LLC would have represented a terrific opportunity to write a strangle.)

On 19 April 1999, I wrote an $18.00 put for a May expiry and received a 20¢ premium. On that day, LLC closed at $20.16. Using candlesticks to guide my entry point, I waited for a turn up from the bottom of the channel in order to maximise my premium. To be exercised, LLC would have to drop $2.16! I felt that this was a 'high probability trade'. LLC's closing price on 27 May 1999, the expiry date, was $19.54, a full $1.54 away from my put strike price.

Fig. 8.1 LEND LEASE DAILY

Created with SuperCharts by Omega Research ® 1997

A BHP CANDLESTICK CLASSIC

Here is an example of writing a put underneath a downtrending share that looked like it was due for a reversal. BHP was in an established, but slow-moving, downtrend (see Fig. 8.2). When a bullish engulfing pattern formed (14/15 December 1998), I could hardly let it pass without acting. I waited for confirmation that BHP had formed a trough for a couple of days to ensure that the share price was going to move up. On 17 December 1998, I wrote out-of-the-money $10.50 puts and received a 25¢ premium. BHP closed at $11.95 on the expiration day, 28 January 1999. I retained the full premium that I received when I wrote the put.

FIG. 8.2 BHP DAILY

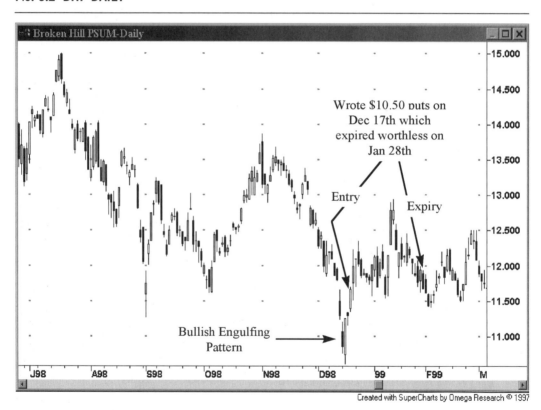

Created with SuperCharts by Omega Research © 1997

BEAT THE CLOCK STRANGLE

(OK I admit it, I have made up this name! But it's effective, so who cares what the strategy is called?)

Just imagine that you have written some out-of-the-money puts earlier in the month and the share trends downward but does not penetrate your put strike. Obviously this is a somewhat nerve-wracking situation. If you have positioned your strike below a significant support/resistance level, it is quite possible that the share will rebound from this line. If it does not penetrate your support/resistance line, then your puts will be safe.

One of the ways to partially cover your risk without closing out your threatened puts is to write a short-term call with only a few days to go prior to expiry. If you believe that you have detected a call strike that will not be penetrated within a few days of expiry, and you can get a sufficient premium; this may be a worthwhile strategy for you. The premium you derive from your written call will assist in covering the put that you will need to close out if your strike is penetrated. If the share does not penetrate your call or your put level, you are playing 'beat the clock' with the amount of time decay you have remaining on both options. Every hour that ticks past within the last few days prior to expiry will lessen your exit costs on either the written call or the written put if the market turns against you.

This strategy is easier to understand when I provide you with an example.

A RIO trade

On 4 May 1999, I wrote RIO puts at a $22.50 strike price and received a 14¢ premium, (see Fig. 8.3). On that day, RIO closed at $25.95 and there were 18 days to go before expiry. The share would have to drop $3.45 within 18 days to threaten my strike.

I decided that the trade represented a calculated risk, as the put strike was positioned two resistance levels away. It was a safe trade, or so I thought. No sooner than I had written the contracts, the share then proceeded to head south. Unfortunately, it seemed that I had failed to recognise a double top! (A double top shows two peaks that are basically symmetrical. It typically signifies that a downtrend is about to begin.) Now I was in the game of 'beat the clock' and with anxious anticipation, I watched time decay eat away the size of the premium that it would cost me to exit the trade. Sometimes in the writing game, even when you have incorrectly analysed a share, it can still lead to a winning trade due to time decay. (Obviously, the goal however, is to get the analysis correct in the first place!)

With five days to expiry, the share price was $23.28. My written puts were still one resistance level away from risk. At this stage, I calculated that it would be unlikely for the share price to go above the $25.00 mark. Therefore, I wrote $25.00 calls and received 8¢ with just five days to expiry! This generated a healthy buffer of premium in case my puts needed to be closed out.

Fig. 8.3 RIO TINTO DAILY

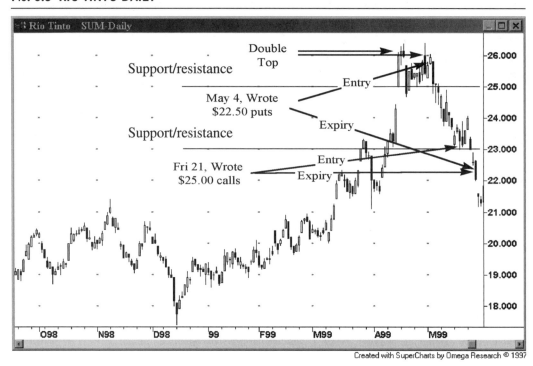

Created with SuperCharts by Omega Research © 1997

In fact, my puts did need to be closed out, as the day before expiry, RIO's price closed at $22.50! Oh no! I closed out my $22.50 puts at 30¢ when RIO was valued at $22.24 on the actual day of expiry. The 30¢ premium represented 26¢ of intrinsic value and 4¢ of time value.

Luckily, I made the decision to close out these puts because RIO's closing price on the 27 May 1999 expiry day was $22.05, $2.45 away from my calls but placing my puts 45¢ in-the-money. I am so glad that I closed out my position in order to avoid being exercised. RIO continued to go down in value the next day, so I was incredibly relieved that I took the defensive action of closing out. Ironically, RIO promptly uptrended strongly, so with the benefit of hindsight, it may have been beneficial to purchase the share after all.

Trading Secrets

Be prepared to alter your initial view of the trend of a share price if it does not continue as expected.

REVIEW

1) If your view of the share is bullish, what writing strategy should you implement? Where should you position your strike price?

2) What is exposure and why is it important when you are considering writing put options? What is your exposure on five BHP put contracts at a $15.00 strike price?

ANSWERS

1) If your view is bullish, then you are likely to write out-of-the-money put options one to two support/resistance levels away from the current share price.

2) Exposure is very important as you need to be financially able to cover any put contracts that you have written. If you have written 5 BHP put contracts at a $15.00 strike price, your exposure is $75,000, (5000 x $15.00 = $75,000). The implication of this is that if you are exercised you need to purchase $75,000 of BHP.

→ → → *Now that you have worked out some lovely option strategies to make some money, what will happen if something goes wrong? Keep reading to learn how you can remove yourself from risk by taking defensive* → → → *actions...*

Chapter Nine

DEFENDING YOUR TURF___

HIT RATE

I have learned the most about trading when I have taken a loss on a trade. I have always found that I learn the lessons of life with amazing clarity if the lesson involves money being taken away from me!

People often ask about my hit rate or proportion of winning trades to losing trades. This hit rate is largely irrelevant because when dealing with options, it really does not matter whether you have 99% of your trades that *win*, if the 1% of your trades that *lose* are not handled well.

"It really does not matter whether you have 99% of your trades that WIN, if the 1% of your trades that LOSE are not handled well."

Every so often, it is wise to look back over your past trades and seek to learn the lessons that history has been trying to teach you. If you have been keeping a trading diary, you can just flick back through the pages and review your trading rationale and results. (Refer to Chapter 13 for more details on how to keep a trading diary.)

The first time that I reviewed my trading history, I noticed a startling fact. The months that I made my biggest losses in options directly followed the months that I had made an amazingly healthy profit! Unfortunately, this sad indictment on my options trading style is very common among other traders also. It seems that after a big win, your ego is likely to increase in direct proportion to your bank balance. This is an extremely dangerous situation from which to trade. Pride comes before a fall!

Preservation of capital must be the underlying goal of all traders. It is important to note that if you make a loss of 10% of your trading capital, you must make an 11.1% return on your next trade just to break even. However, if you make a 50% loss in trading capital, you will need to make a 100% profit on your next trade to break even! This is a lesson which seems to escape many traders. In regard to writing options, your returns are usually small and fixed in value, however, your losses can be exponential in nature if not carefully managed. The separation between effective traders and amateurs largely lies in their money management skills.

Trading Secrets

Without effective defensive actions, one losing written options trade can be financially devastating.

WHAT ARE DEFENSIVE ACTIONS?

Defensive actions act as a last resort when the share goes against the view you had when you initially wrote the option. You will often incur a loss when using a defensive action, but this may be preferable to being exercised and incurring a far greater loss. You need to weigh the risks carefully. Also, consider peace of mind, as this may be the greatest reason for taking a defensive action and limiting your risk. At least if you are no longer in a trade that is causing you stress, you can sleep at night without fear of what the morning trading may bring!

Often when writing puts and naked calls, the aim is not to get exercised. If you are exercised on a contract, you need to remember that this may not be the best time, technically, to perform this trade. For example, if you are exercised on a put contract, the indicators may be showing a sell situation, instead of a buy. If you are exercised on a put option where all indicators are screaming *'get the heck out of this share'* you may be forced to buy a share that would not qualify according to your usual share purchasing rules. Of course, you could allow yourself to be exercised and then immediately sell the share you have just purchased on the open market. However, if you follow this course of action, the brokerage and slippage in share price that you may experience could make this a very expensive proposition.

In this situation, it would be wise to remove yourself from risk by implementing one of the many defensive actions that are available. In this chapter I discuss these defensive actions, and provide some guidance about when to desert the sinking ship. Personally, I do not like the game of Russian roulette, so if I am concerned that I will be exercised, I take defensive action to remove myself from risk.

Let's have a look at how contracts get exercised. As an option buyer, once you inform your broker of your desire to exercise, contracts in that strike price are randomly selected by the OCH. Just imagine that three buyers decide to exercise their rights, and there are a total of ten contracts available at that strike price. Metaphorically speaking, the OCH will dip three times into a hat that contains ten contracts. So even if you have written an option at that strike price, you may be exercised, or you may be lucky and avoid being exercised. It is also possible to be exercised on part of your total options contract. For example, one out of the seven contracts that you have written may be exercised.

Some of the trades in the examples that I have provided lead to loss or break-even situations. Rather than just giving you a selection of winning trades, it is important that you begin to understand some of the consequences of incorrect analysis, and how you can remove yourself from risky situations.

SHARE PRICE AND OPTION PREMIUMS

For a put option, as the share price goes up, the price of the put premium for that strike price goes down, (see Table 9.1). This is because the written put option at that particular strike price is now at less risk of being exercised. If the share price drops however, your puts are more at risk, so the premiums for these puts increase in direct proportion to their level of risk.

For a call option, as the share price goes down, the price of the call premium for that strike price goes down, (see Table 9.1). The less risk of being exercised means that the premiums also decrease. However, as a share price goes up, your written calls will be threatened, so the premiums will increase.

Table 9.1 THE EFFECT OF SHARE PRICE CHANGES ON OPTION PREMIUMS

As the share price goes up:

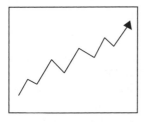

CALL OPTION PREMIUMS	PUT OPTION PREMIUMS
Go Up	Go Down

As the share price goes down:

CALL OPTION PREMIUMS	PUT OPTION PREMIUMS
Go Down	Go Up

This is a key principle that explains why taking a more aggressive option position leads to higher premiums. It also explains why you are likely to take a loss when you implement a defensive action, (and why option buyers can make incredible profits if they trade with the trend).

You may remember that you 'Sell to Open' your initial option writing transaction. When writing options, you actually receive money from the option buyer. (This definitely adds to the appeal of writing options!) Because you have opened the position by selling, it makes sense to close a position by buying, doesn't it?

I realise that this sounds obscure, initially, but it is reasons like this that stop the average trader from conquering the options writing market. The persistent few who conquer these concepts are the ones who create wealth using these methods.

If your calls are threatened, what can you do?

ROLLING UP

If you are exercised on a written call option, you must deliver shares to the option taker. Let's have a look at the situation on a transaction basis (disregarding any brokerage fees, etc.). It is as if the selling price of the share is the strike price plus the price of the premium you received when you wrote the option. For example, imagine that you have written a $14.00 call and received a 20¢ premium. If you are exercised, although you are selling the share for $14.00, it is as if you are selling your share for $14.20 (because of this 20¢ buffer). You need to carefully consider whether you would like to be exercised, or whether an alternative action would be preferable.

If you have written a call and the market rallies past your strike price, you can roll up. Rolling up involves closing out your initial call option position, and opening another at a higher strike price, (see Fig. 9.1). This may allow you to avoid being exercised if you do not wish to deliver shares to the option taker at that strike price. By seeking a higher strike, you are rolling away from the risk represented at your initial strike. You may incur a loss, however this may be preferable to being exercised.

Fig. 9.1 BHP DAILY

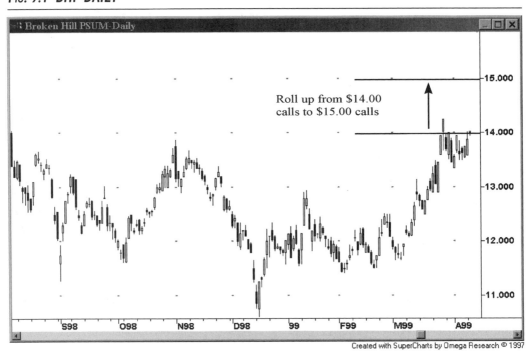

Roll up from $14.00 calls to $15.00 calls

Created with SuperCharts by Omega Research © 1997

The actual cost of the roll will need to be calculated to keep your profit/loss records intact. To calculate your profit/loss, calculate the amount of money that you made when you sold to open the position, then subtract the amount of money it took you to close the deal. Finally, add on the amount of money you received by opening the new position at the higher strike price. Remember to subtract any costs incurred, e.g. brokerage, fees from the OCH, etc.

Does this sound confusing? Imagine the position that your broker will be in if he/she does not understand your intentions. You may find that your instructions were not acted on simply because of a miscommunication. It is always wise to use the correct terminology, especially when closing old and then opening new positions. Here is the correct terminology as well as the profit/loss calculations, to use as an example.

TERMINOLOGY

Sell to open 5 BHP December 'xx $14.00 call contracts at 20¢.

Buy to close 5 BHP December 'xx $14.00 call contracts at 50¢.

Sell to open 5 BHP December 'xx $15.00 call contracts at 19¢.

The actual cost of this roll would be calculated as follows:

Sell to open 5000 x 20¢ = $1000

Buy to close 5000 x 50¢ = ($2500)

Sell to open 5000 x 19¢ = $950

Actual Loss = ($550) (excluding costs).

Trading Secrets

If a written call is in danger of being exercised, you can roll up by closing the initial written call, and then write new calls at a higher strike price.

ROLLING DOWN

If you are exercised on a written put option, you must buy the shares covered by the contract. I will have a look at the situation on a transaction basis (disregarding any brokerage fees, etc.). In this example, it is as if the purchase price of the share is the strike price minus the price of the premium you received when you wrote the option. Imagine that you have written a $12.00 put for a 10¢ premium, and you are exercised. Although you are buying the share for $12.00, it is as if you are buying it for $11.90 (because of this 10¢ buffer). This is because you have already factored the premium that you have received into the equation. The premium creates a buffer when considering the share purchase price. You need to carefully consider whether you would like to be exercised and buy the shares, or whether an alternative action would be preferable. One of the defensive actions available in this situation is to roll down.

If you have written a put and the market downtrends and threatens your strike, you can roll down. This method allows you to close out your initial written put position, and open another at a lower strike price, (see Fig. 9.2). Rolling down allows you to avoid being exercised if you do not wish to purchase the shares at that strike price. You may incur a loss, however this may be preferable to being exercised.

TERMINOLOGY

Sell to open 5 BHP December 'xx $12.00 put contracts at 10¢.

Buy to close 5 BHP December 'xx $12.00 put contracts at 45¢.

Sell to open 5 BHP December 'xx $11.00 put contracts at 15¢.

The actual cost of this roll would be calculated as follows:

Sell to open 5000 x 10¢ = $500

Buy to close 5000 x 45¢ = ($2250)

Sell to open 5000 x 15¢ = $750

Actual Loss = ($1000) (excluding costs).

FIG. 9.2 BHP DAILY

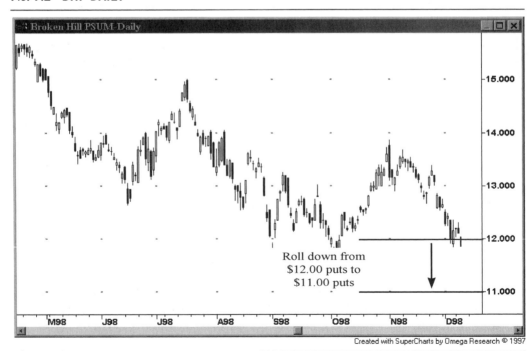

Roll down from
$12.00 puts to
$11.00 puts

Created with SuperCharts by Omega Research © 1997

Trading Secrets

You could roll down on threatened written put positions by closing out your initial position and opening another at a lower strike price.

ROLLING OUT

If you have written a put or a call and the market trends past your strike price, you can roll out to a later month. This method allows you to close out your initial trade, and open another at a later expiry date and/or a different strike price, in order to avoid being exercised. In this situation, it is probable that you may actually profit on the defensive action because you are accepting a position with greater inherent risk due to the increased time value in the new position.

Can you live with the extra time risk that this strategy involves? You were incorrect in your analysis once, so what makes you think you will be correct if you give yourself more time? If you can answer these questions (honestly) and still feel that this is the correct strategy for your situation, then you could roll out. If you have written *covered* calls, you can be more flexible, and roll out to a later date if you feel that this is appropriate.

In my view, the easy route of rolling out on naked positions allows you to become less disciplined as a trader. Subconsciously, you are allowing an incorrectly analysed trade to provide a potential profit (as you are likely, but not certain, to make money on a rolling out strategy).

A trading success is often largely based on the discipline and skill of the individual. By allowing yourself to avoid punishment and taking a profit where you should be taking a loss, you are rewarding yourself for poor performance.

In many ways, I believe the best method is to take it on the chin and close out as described on the following page.

However, if you would still like to roll out and accept more time risk, then at least use the correct terminology.

TERMINOLOGY

Sell to open 5 BHP October 'xx $14.00 call contracts at 15¢.
Buy to close 5 BHP October 'xx $14.00 call contracts at 45¢.
Sell to open 5 BHP December 'xx $14.00 call contracts at 65¢.

The actual cost/profit of this roll would be calculated as follows:

Sell to open 5000 x 15¢ = $750
Buy to close 5000 x 45¢ = ($2250)
Sell to open 5000 x 65¢ = $3250
Actual Profit = $1750 (excluding costs).

Trading Secrets

▸ *You could roll out by opening a position at a later expiry date.*

▸ *Closing out is my preferred strategy.*

CLOSING OUT

Closing out is my preferred strategy, particularly for short-dated option contracts. You may need to implement a closing out strategy if the strike prices of your written put or call options are threatened.

When taking this course of defensive action, you will incur a loss as the share has turned against your initial view. With rolling strategies, you have the benefit of recouping some of your loss as you open a new, less risky, position.

If you choose to close out then feel proud that you have taken a loss with grace. You have just joined the ranks of the professional traders who have learned to take their losses with little emotion.

TERMINOLOGY

Sell to open 5 BHP August 'xx $14.50 puts at 15¢.
Buy to close 5 BHP August 'xx $14.50 puts at 50¢.

The actual cost of this roll would be calculated as follows:

Sell to open 5000 x 15¢ = $750
Buy to close 5000 x 50¢ = ($2500)
Actual Loss = ($1750) (excluding costs).

Summary of Terminology

To open a position:	Sell to open 5 BHP September 'xx $18.00 call contracts at 10¢.
	Sell to open 5 BHP August 'xx $12.00 put contracts at 30¢.
To close:	Buy to close 5 BHP September 'xx $18.00 call contracts at 30¢.
	Buy to close 5 BHP August 2000 $12.00 put contracts at 45¢.
To roll:	Buy to close 5 BHP August 'xx $12.00 put contracts at 45¢.
	Sell to open 5 BHP September 'xx $11.00 put contracts at 20¢.

Always use the correct terminology when speaking with your broker!

Why am I so hung up on terminology? Let me tell you about an experience that I had which emphasised the importance of using the correct wording.

When my broker left his previous brokerage firm, I still had a few option trades open before I transferred all of my business to his new place of employment. One of my BHP put trades was threatened and I needed to close out immediately. I rang the new broker assigned to my account and I said that I would like to "Buy to close 7 BHP December 'xx $12.00 put contracts at market price". The new broker sounded confident and she assured me that she knew all about the options market. Satisfied, I placed my order and rang back in the afternoon to be told that my order had been filled. I slept well that night, as I knew that I had removed myself from a potentially very damaging situation.

Within two days, the paperwork from this trade arrived in the mail. To my horror, I realised that this new broker had 'Sold to Open' instead of 'Bought to Close'. With utter dismay, I looked at the current price of the put option in the newspaper and I saw that I was facing a $7000 loss. My small loss of $500 had magnified into a $7000 loss because of a mistake made by the broker!

After pointing out this grievous error, I learned that my conversation was on tape with that brokerage firm. If I had not used the exact terminology required to close out my position, I probably would have had to absorb that loss. Because I had used the specific terminology required, the brokerage firm was under obligation to assume responsibility for the error!

SUGGESTIONS

When rolling down or up or out, only roll once—EVER!

Take your punishment and learn from your mistakes. Do not keep compounding your error and let your pride prevent you from getting out of a potentially damaging situation! Would you rather be right or rich? If you hang around until you are proved right by the share price, you are likely to have seriously damaged your cash reserves. There is no room for that kind of pride in trading.

In my view, closing out is preferable to rolling. I like to follow my discipline and take it on the chin if I have been wrong. In addition, rolling up or down is preferable to rolling out. I choose to roll up or down within the same month where my new strike price will be one or two resistance/support levels away from the share price. This situation does not occur very often, so mostly, if in doubt, close it out!

Rolling down your written puts is, in many ways, similar to being caught in the path of an avalanche. If the avalanche is cascading down the mountain and you are in its way, you have two choices. Either you could be airlifted to safety, (you close out), or you can run like the wind down the mountain. If you can outrun the avalanche, then you will survive. However, if the avalanche comes down on top of you... the effects could be disastrous.

Look for opportunities to close out written put positions from an early stage in the month. If you have made a handsome profit in just a few days, and another opportunity beckons, why not close out a winning trade for a profit? Usually I conduct a four-week strategy (broken down into the weeks of the month) with expiry being in the final week. If I have made a 75% profit on the premium by week two in the month, I take the profit and run. For example, if my initial premium was 20¢ and I can subsequently close out the position for 5¢, then I will. In the second week of the month there may still be some attractive opportunities for an end-of-the-month expiry. My exposure would be considerably less so I am likely to jump into another promising trade. This is the main benefit of a steeply trending share in the options market as opposed to a sideways trading share.

You should close out on written puts more aggressively than on written calls. This is because puts are more likely to be exercised prior to expiry and there is always the risk of a correction.

If you decide to give your trade a little more time to prove itself, it is possible to wait until the expiry day and close out in the final hour if necessary. The benefit here is that the time value of the option is minimal, and the intrinsic value will closely approximate the closing out price. The market makers or registered traders are the intermediaries between the brokers and the market. They set the price of the option. Because the market makers are in the business of making money, they will take a few cents for themselves in order to cover their efforts, so the intrinsic value will not always be the same as your exit premium in the final hour of the expiry day. For example, the premium may be quoted as 1¢, but to actually close out your position, the market maker may charge you 3¢.

Market makers have a vested interest to exercise any in- or at-the-money options on the expiry day. They often implement strategies which are effective, regardless of in which direction the market is moving, so it is essential to be aware that they are another spoke in the wheel of the options market.

An NCP Example

Here is a strangle that went horribly wrong for me. You are about see a real life defensive action.

In April 1999 I performed a strangle on NCP, a particularly volatile stock, (see Fig. 9.3). The share was in a flat trading band when a fundamental factor came into play. The stock took a massive Herculean leap right over my written call strike price of $13.00. Luckily I had written puts underneath the share at $10.50 which provided a little consolation as these were now no longer at any risk.

The strike price of my written calls had been penetrated by greater than the premium I received when I initially opened the position. I decided that a quick, but graceful, exit was essential. I closed out the trade the next day and took a nasty loss. However, the fact that I was out of the position let me sleep soundly that night. If I hadn't closed out at that stage, I would have dreaded each passing day of share price increase as my losses would have been mounting significantly.

Ironically, the closing price of the share on the expiry day was less than my call strike. This meant that unless I had been exercised early on in the position, there was a good chance that I had taken an unnecessary defensive action. However, I would rather jump out of a worrying trade than hold on and hope that my losses were not going to be catastrophic.

Fɪɢ. *9.3 NEWS CORPORATION DAILY*

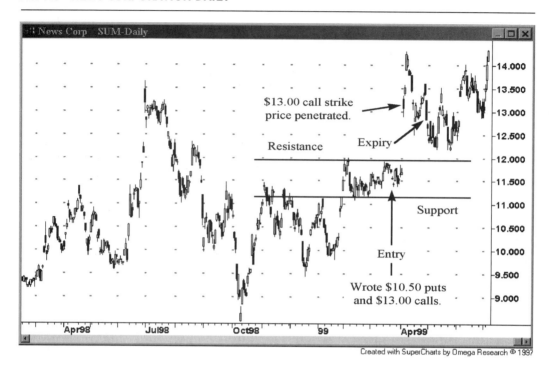

→ → → **Now that you have seen some specific option writing strategies and defensive actions, let's look at one of the most important aspects of trading this market, the impact of dividends on options...** → → →

Chapter Ten

THE DIVIDEND

EFFECT

A dividend is part of a company's net profit that is paid to shareholders as a cash reward for investing in the company's shares. This periodic profit payment to the shareholders is often made on a quarterly basis. It is usually paid out as a number of cents per share. Companies that are performing well typically pay dividends in excess of their non-performing counterparts.

When the market is preparing for a dividend payment, the share price often increases in value. Demand increases due to the promise of a dividend payment. Once a stock goes ex-dividend, the price of the share often *falls* dramatically.

It is essential that you take the time to understand the impact of this drop in share price on the options market. When a share drops in price, your written calls become *less* risky. The share price has moved away from the call strike price in a positive manner. Consequently, your call premiums for each particular strike price will decrease in value.

A share price drop may jeopardise your written puts. Due to this *increased risk* factor, after a share has gone ex-dividend, your put premiums will increase in value. The share price is now closer to, or may have penetrated, your written put strike price.

As is evident, fluctuating share prices have major implications in relation to both your written calls and written puts. Any dramatic overnight drop in share price will form a gap down in the price action of the chart. There are several types of gaps that may be evident when viewing a chart. These are often described as a 'sucker's gap', a 'false gap' and a 'real gap'.

A sucker's gap is when a share goes ex-dividend and the corresponding share drop is visible in the chart. You need to know the ex-dividend date in advance in order to observe the subsequent gap in the share price.

False gaps occur without an accompanying volume increase.

A real gap in a share chart has an associated increase in volume.

In general, there are three types of real gaps. A breakaway gap is a big gap on heavy volume at the start of a trend. A continuation or a runaway gap mostly leads to prices continuing in the direction of the trend. An exhaustion gap may indicate that a trend is running out of puff and that a change in the direction of the trend may occur, (see Fig 10.1).

FIG. 10.1 NEWS CORPORATION DAILY

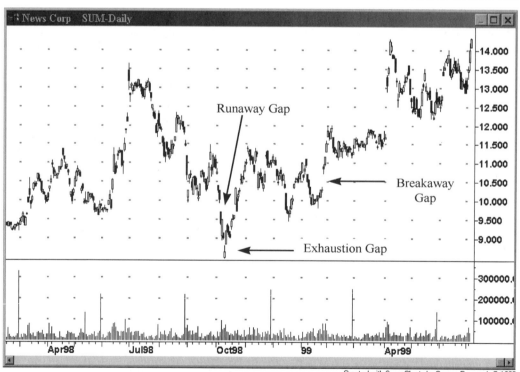

Created with SuperCharts by Omega Research © 1997

How Much will the Share Price Drop When it Goes Ex-dividend?

This is an important question to consider when trading options. In order to assess this, the first question that you need to ask is whether the dividend is fully franked or unfranked. Fully franked, or partially franked, dividends mean that the company has paid tax on the dividend before you receive it. This makes it possible for you to pay less tax on income from shares due to dividend imputation tax credits.

Unfranked dividends are considered to be of less value to shareholders. With unfranked dividends, the shareholder must shoulder the full tax burden. The level of franking has important implications in regard to the ultimate share price drop that the share will display after it goes ex-dividend.

As a rough guide, for unfranked dividends, the share falls by approximately the price of the declared dividend. Fully franked dividends historically show a share price decrease of many more cents than the declared dividend. Although the corresponding share drop will also depend on market conditions, here are some general guidelines that may provide a basis for your calculations. It is wise to be conservative in your estimates and consider the worst case scenario if your calculations do not come to fruition.

From my observation, the corresponding drop in share price for a fully franked dividend will usually be between 20% and 60% *in excess* of the declared dividend price. To make calculations simple, perhaps use 50% in excess of the declared dividend as a guide. For example, a fully franked dividend of 50¢ per share may result in a share price drop of 75¢.

This rule does not always hold true, but serves to provide a sound estimate of share price activity in an ex-dividend situation. In times of heightened volatility, the effect of this phenomenon will vary. During rapid sharemarket rallies, the ex-dividend share price drop could be less than this amount. The converse is also true. In bear market conditions, the ex-dividend drop may be accentuated.

For partially franked dividends, you need to calculate the share price drop by taking the percentage of franking into account. For example, a 75% franking on a 50¢ dividend may result in a share price drop of approximately 68¢. This is calculated as follows:

50¢ x 50% = 25¢

75% (franking) of 25¢ = 18¢

50¢ + 18¢ = 68¢

Therefore, the approximate drop in share price will be 68¢.

Despite this observation of falls in the share price, it is important that you satisfy yourself on this issue by monitoring the ex-dividend share gaps over time. Although there are many examples that fulfil the above theory of share price drops, there are several occasions when the share price does not behave in such a predictable manner.

When NAB went ex-dividend on 8 June 2000, the dividend was 59¢ fully franked. The actual corresponding share price drop on 9 June was 84¢. This was due to the tax implications of fully franked dividends; 59¢ + (0.50 x 59¢) = an expected drop of approximately 88¢.

However, the share price decrease for ANZ when it went ex-dividend on 7 June 1999 was considerably less. The dividend for ANZ at that time was 26¢, 75% franked. The closing price on the day prior to the ex-dividend date was $11.18, however the opening price was only 4¢ lower on 7 June (even though it closed at $10.86 on that day). The fact that the DOW had increased by over 150 points overnight possibly had an effect on this ex-dividend situation, (see Fig. 10.2).

Fɪɢ. 10.2 ANZ DAILY

Created with SuperCharts by Omega Research © 1997

As another observation, for uptrending shares, the ex-dividend share price gap often recovers within five to seven trading days. The gap closes as the subsequent price activity continues its upward trend. In the case of downtrending shares, the share price sometimes does not recover. You have to be aware of the trend of the share to estimate the changes in share price after an ex-dividend situation.

Each share does not always go ex-dividend on the same day each year. You can keep track of the ex-dividend dates by monitoring your newspaper or asking your broker.

To some extent the effect of the dividend is factored into option premiums, however it is still important to be aware of the strategic implications. Now that you know the theory, it is time to have a closer look at the ex-dividend implications in relation to call and put options.

Call Options

Most call option buyers exercise at, or close to, expiry. A major reason to exercise is to obtain shares from the option writer before the share has gone ex-dividend. The buyer is likely to be thinking: 'Why not purchase the share prior to it going ex-dividend and prior to expiry in order to enjoy the added benefit of receiving a dividend?' In this situation, buyers have a vested interest in exercising their call options.

As a writer, you can play this scenario to your advantage by writing calls over the top of a stock that goes ex-dividend close to the expiry date of the option. This will assist you in maximising your chances for success of the trade. It is very likely that the share price will drop on the ex-dividend date and that your open position has become less risky overnight.

Put Options

Buyers are more likely to want to exercise earlier on a put than on a call option. This allows them to free up capital by selling their shares to the option writer so that they can participate in another opportunity in the market. The other major reason to exercise is to 'dump' shares onto the option writer after the share has gone ex-dividend and the characteristic share drop in value has broken through, or is close to the put strike price. The buyer has a personal stake in selling his shares to the writer, after he has 'stripped' out the dividend.

Draft legislation has been put forward regarding dividend imputation. Shareholders must now hold a share for more than 45 days (90 days for preference shares) in order to benefit from the dividend franking credits.

Despite this legislation, it is still important to be aware that the put buyer has a vested interest in exercising after an ex-dividend situation.

As a put writer, you need to ensure that the share does not drop through your strike price as it goes ex-dividend. You could choose to write puts under a share that is going ex-dividend, but then implement a closing out strategy prior to the ex-dividend date if you believe your strike price will be threatened. Prior to the ex-dividend date, when the share price is higher, the put premiums will be lower than after the share drops in price. This represents an ideal exit point from your trade if you estimate that your written puts may be penetrated. If in doubt, close it out!

If you have located an uptrending share, then you could maximise your premiums by writing puts underneath the share, after it has gone ex-dividend. In all probability, the uptrending share price will recover within five to seven days after it has experienced an ex-dividend share price drop. This will assist in removing your written puts from risk.

There are a few points to consider if you have implemented a strangle strategy on a share that is going ex-dividend. To refresh your memory, a strangle strategy is where you write a call over and a put under the same share at different strike prices. The aim is to have both your written calls and puts expire worthless.

A conservative strangle would have both the call and put strikes out-of-the-money (i.e. your written calls above the share price, and your written puts below).

Be aware that a close-to-the-money strangle has higher levels of risk in an ex-dividend situation. You will need to take particular care that the call price is not penetrated prior to the share going ex-dividend, or you may be exercised. In addition, you may be exercised on your written puts if the share drops through your strike price. In other words, you may get exercised on both your written calls and puts within two subsequent days!

As you can see, ex-dividend dates have important implications for both call and put options whether buying or writing. It is not necessary to avoid writing options on shares that are going ex-dividend. However, it is absolutely essential to be aware of the implications and levels of vested interest that the buyers will have to exercise their rights. As a suggestion, it may pay to implement a more conservative strategy for calls and puts during this ex-dividend time, particularly if you are new to writing options.

Trading Secrets

Ex-dividend situations represent exciting opportunities for writing both call and put options.

➔ ➔   ➔ *By now, you will have started to accumulate a lot of knowledge about the options writing game. In the next chapter, you will have an opportunity to test your skills by performing an actual trade…*➔ ➔ ➔

Chapter Eleven

THE OPTIONS GAME

Y ou are at an exciting stage of the learning curve. You are ready to implement your newfound knowledge by playing a very special game.

Rather than investing your hard-earned dollars without having any experience in the options market, this section of the book is designed to give you a chance to assess your knowledge and place some 'actual' trades (without the risk of losing money). By taking the time to complete this game, you will definitely pinpoint the areas that require more work prior to placing a real options order. Take the exercises seriously and you will learn valuable lessons about your options trading style. There is no 'right' answer to the game. You will need to assess each position carefully, as there are no magic answers at the end of the chapter. This will be more beneficial to you than handing you the answers on a plate. Take your time and enjoy the ride!

During the game, you may need to refresh your memory on certain sections of the preceding chapters. I would rather you take the chance to review these sections instead of jumping into an inappropriate trading position.

SCOPE OF THE GAME

➲ After analysing the share, you may find that you are unwilling to open any written option positions due to the risk involved, or that the premium available is too low. This is totally valid, and I suggest that in real life you do not look to open trades that are inappropriate. By looking to trade where the conditions are not ideal, you are opening yourself up to unacceptable levels of risk. However, for the sake of learning the lessons inherent in this game, I suggest that you place at least one order for each round of this paper trade.

⊃ To restrict the scope of this exercise, it is necessary to open a short-term written options position with only one month until expiry. In real life, you will have a greater opportunity to choose the term of your position.

⊃ Please note that no share in this exercise is due to go ex-dividend.

⊃ Assume you do not own any shares when you are playing the game, so any puts or calls that you write will be uncovered, or naked.

⊃ Usually I open my positions in week one of the month and continue monitoring these positions every day until expiry. To play this game, you will have the opportunity to monitor your positions less frequently than you would in real life. Nevertheless, the chance to paper trade and examine the effect of the share price on option premiums is most useful.

⊃ You will have the chance to open positions based on two share charts. This obviously imposes a restricted focus.

⊃ I suggest that you record a premium that is halfway between the bid and the ask. For example, if the buyer's column shows 12¢ and the seller's column shows 16¢, then you should record 14¢ as the premium that you were able to attain.

⊃ The only defensive actions available in this game are to roll up or down or to close out. I have not supplied rolling out as an available choice.

GUIDELINES

In summary, these following six points can provide a basis for writing options:

1) What is your view of the trend of the share? What is the duration of this trend? (In real life, remember to take into account the effect of any share ex-dividend dates.)

2) Write calls for downtrending/lateral shares, or beyond the price that you believe the share will reach by expiry if the upward movement appears to be running out of momentum.

3) Write puts for uptrending/lateral shares or beyond the price that you believe the share will reach by expiry if the downward movement appears to be running out of momentum.

4) Decide how many contracts you would like to write based on the level of exposure with which you are comfortable and can handle financially. For the sake of the game, make the number of contracts that you choose as realistic as possible.

5) Monitor your positions.

6) Take defensive action if necessary.

You are now ready to play the Options Game...

THE OPTIONS GAME

Round 1

1) Imagine that you are currently within week one of July 1999. By opening your options positions with the NAB on a Thursday or a Friday, you are utilising the time decay of the option wisely. (Remember with time decay, you are hoping to sell the buyer a rapidly depreciating asset. As time decay also applies to the weekend, the best time to write options is on a Thursday or a Friday.)

You need to look closely at the weekly share chart, (Fig. 11.1), the daily share chart, (Fig. 11.2), and Options Table, (Table 11.1), on Wednesday of week one, in order to prepare your analysis prior to placing your orders on the Thursday or Friday. Follow each of the steps listed, noting your answers in the space provided. This will assist in clarifying your view, prior to opening a position.

Table 11.1 OPTIONS TABLE WEEK ONE

CALL OPTIONS   **Wednesday 8 July 1999**

Stock	Strike Price	Buyer	Seller	Last Sale	T.O. 000	Open Int.
NAB Last Sale Price $25.05 1999						
Jul	24.50	.98	1.08	1.11		104
Jul	25.00	.69	.79	.73	12	2926
Jul	25.50	.50	.55	.56	53	1213
Jul	26.00	.32	.38	.35	130	3236
Jul	26.50	.18	.23	.20	105	2406
Jul	27.00	.10	.16	.10	460	2645
Jul	27.50	.06	.10	.04	590	2805
Jul	28.00	.02	.06	.07	5	2281

PUT OPTIONS   **Wednesday 8 July 1999**

Stock	Strike Price	Buyer	Seller	Last Sale	T.O. 000	Open Int.
NAB Last Sale Price $25.05 1999						
Jul	22.50	.01	.06	.35		34
Jul	23.00	.02	.10	.10		1350
Jul	23.50	.06	.16	.14	10	181
Jul	24.00	.12	.28	.23	45	1915
Jul	24.50	.22	.44	.36	9	833
Jul	25.00	.36	.65	.61	37	1873
Jul	25.50	.57	.94	.87	80	727
Jul	26.00	.84	1.26	1.03		2087

➲ Analyse the share by drawing in trendlines, support and resistance lines, and observing the moving averages. Is your view bullish, bearish or is the share trending sideways?

Fig. 11.1 NATIONAL AUSTRALIA BANK WEEKLY

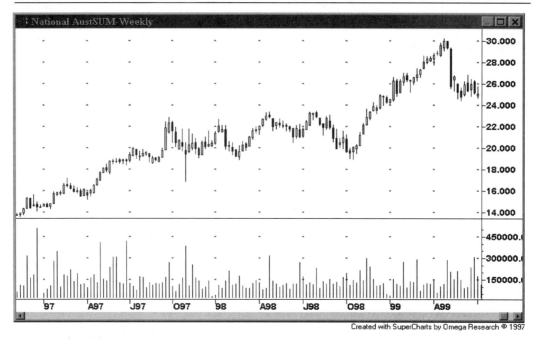

Created with SuperCharts by Omega Research ® 1997

Fig. 11.2 NATIONAL AUSTRALIA BANK DAILY

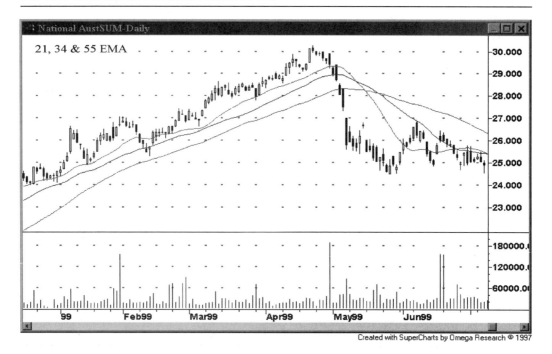

Created with SuperCharts by Omega Research ® 1997

➲ Do you want to write calls, puts or perform a strangle strategy for an end of the month expiry?

_____

_____

➲ Where will you position your strike price(s)?

_____

_____

➲ Record the correct terminology to open your position.

_____

_____

2) *Time has passed and you are in week two of July. Review the share chart, (see Fig 11.3). Have a look at the current options section of the newspaper, (see Table 11.2) and note the premiums available now on your written option positions. (If your chosen strike price is not included in this options table, it is likely that the premium has now been reduced to a negligible level, e.g. one cent. If this is the case, you have done very well indeed! Remember that our goal is to have the written option at that strike price expire worthless.)*

Table 11.2 OPTIONS TABLE WEEK TWO

CALL OPTIONS   **Friday 16 July 1999**

Stock	Strike Price	Buyer	Seller	Last Sale	T.O. 000	Open Int.
NAB Last Sale Price $24.15						
1999						
Jul	24.50	.32	.35	.31	85	300
Jul	25.00	.17	.22	.20	10	3087
Jul	25.50	.08	.12	.13	6	1587
Jul	26.00	.04	.07	.07		3446
Jul	26.50	.03	.04	.07	9	2402
Jul	27.00	.02	.04	.05	11	2399
Jul	27.50	.01	.04	.04		2798

PUT OPTIONS

Friday 16 July 1999

Stock	Strike Price	Buyer	Seller	Last Sale	T.O. 000	Open Int.
NAB Last Sale Price $24.15						
1999						
Jul	22.50	.02	.06	.07		59
Jul	23.00	.09	.12	.12		1456
Jul	23.50	.22	.24	.24	40	274
Jul	24.00	.39	.43	.43	764	2035
Jul	24.50	.62	.71	.66	110	922
Jul	25.00	.97	1.04	1.03	41	1839
Jul	25.50	1.36	1.48	1.48	5	729
Jul	26.00	1.80	1.92	1.85	214	2157

Fig. 11.3 NATIONAL AUSTRALIA BANK DAILY

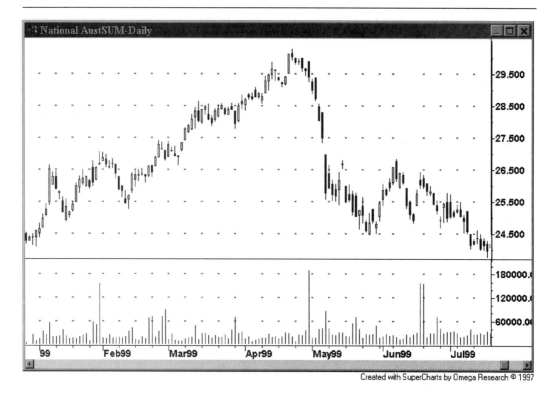

Created with SuperCharts by Omega Research ® 1997

➲ Has the share price gone up or down? Has the premium gone down or up in response to the share price change?

_____

_____

➲ Based on the share price and option premiums in week two, determine whether you will take any defensive actions. If you are going to perform a defensive action, will you roll up, down, or simply close out? If you need to perform a defensive action, record the correct terminology and your existing profit/loss position for this transaction.

_____

_____

3) *You are now in week three of the month and only one week remains before our written option position expires. This will be your last opportunity to take defensive actions prior to expiry. Review Table 11.3 and the share chart in Fig. 11.4*

Table 11.3 OPTIONS TABLE WEEK THREE

| CALL OPTIONS | | | | | | Friday 23 July 1999 |

Stock	Strike Price	Buyer	Seller	Last Sale	T.O. 000	Open Int.
NAB Last Sale Price $24.78						
1999						
Jul	24.50	.49	.57	.54	243	618
Jul	25.00		.47	.27	426	2880
Jul	25.50	.11	.20	.12	391	1562
Jul	26.00	.01	.07	.07	191	3292
Jul	26.50	.02	.05	.06	10	2403
Jul	27.00		.05	.02	14	2442

PUT OPTIONS

Friday 23 July 1999

Stock	Strike Price	Buyer	Seller	Last Sale	T.O. 000	Open Int.
NAB Last Sale Price $24.78						
1999						
Jul	23.50	.03		.03	15	427
Jul	24.00	.07	.11	.12	39	1853
Jul	24.50	.19	.25	.20	281	894
Jul	25.00	.42	.46	.44	214	1772
Jul	25.50	.40		.68	40	707
Jul	26.00	1.19	1.29	1.10	11	1979

FIG. 11.4 NATIONAL AUSTRALIA BANK DAILY

Created with SuperCharts by Omega Research © 1997

➲ Has the premium gone down or up in response to the share price change?

➲ If you are going to perform a defensive action, will you roll up, down, or simply close out?

_____

➲ If you need to perform a defensive action, record the correct terminology and your existing profit/loss position for this transaction:

_____

_____

4) *It is now the day after the expiry day. Have a look at the share price activity on the chart, (see Fig. 11.5) and the option section from the newspaper, (see Table 11.4) with data taken from the day of expiry. How did you go? Was your written position out-of-the-money on the expiry day? If it was, you did very well! You can keep the premium that you received when you first wrote the option. (I'll send a courier over straight away with a bag of money!)*

Table 11.4 OPTIONS TABLE EXPIRY DAY

| CALL OPTIONS | | | | | | Friday 30 July 1999 |

Stock	Strike Price	Buyer	Seller	Last Sale	T.O. 000	Open Int.
NAB Last Sale Price $23.99						
1999						
Jul	23.00	.94	1.04	2.25		24
Jul	23.50	.45	.53	.48	10	70
Jul	24.00		.03	.005	306	303
Jul	24.50		.01	.01	30	836
Jul	25.00		.01	.03	10	2919

| PUT OPTIONS | | | | | | Friday 30 July 1999 |

Stock	Strike Price	Buyer	Seller	Last Sale	T.O. 000	Open Int.
NAB Last Sale Price $23.99						
1999						
Jul	24.00	.01	.02	.01	1228	1894
Jul	24.50	.47	.55	.53	311	1021
Jul	25.00			.93	557	1767
Jul	25.50	1.45	1.57	1.45	3	778
Jul	26.00	1.94	2.08	1.92	245	2262

Fig. 11.5 NATIONAL AUSTRALIA BANK DAILY

Created with SuperCharts by Omega Research ® 1997

➲   If your option was in-the-money on the expiry day, of course, it would have been exercised. Were you happy for this to happen? Should you have taken defensive action earlier in the month? Did you make a loss? What did you learn from this exercise?

_____

_____

⊃   Well done for playing Round 1 of the Options Game. Round 2 now awaits you...

Round 2

1)   *Imagine that you are currently within week one of July 1999. Have a close look at the AMP options table, (Table 11.5), the weekly share chart, (see Fig. 11.6), and the AMP daily share chart, (see Fig. 11.7).*

Table 11.5 OPTIONS TABLE WEEK ONE

CALL OPTIONS   **Wednesday 7 July 1999**

Stock	Strike Price	Buyer	Seller	Last Sale	T.O. 000	Open Int.
AMP Last Sale Price $17.06						
1999						
Jul	16.00	1.10	1.24	.90		411
Jul	16.50	.71	.82	.62	20	489
Jul	17.00	.40	.48	.47	72	775
Jul	17.50	.20	.30	.24	49	774
Jul	18.00	.08	.14	.08	3	139
Jul	18.50	.02	.08	.04		58

PUT OPTIONS   **Wednesday 7 July 1999**

Stock	Strike Price	Buyer	Seller	Last Sale	T.O. 000	Open Int.
AMP Last Sale Price $17.06						
1999						
Jul	16.00	.04	.10	.07	50	271
Jul	16.50	.13	.19	.16	110	566
Jul	17.00	.30	.36	.32	35	351
Jul	17.50	.57	.69	.74	3	144
Jul	18.00	.94	1.08	2.44		20

FIG. 11.6 AMP WEEKLY

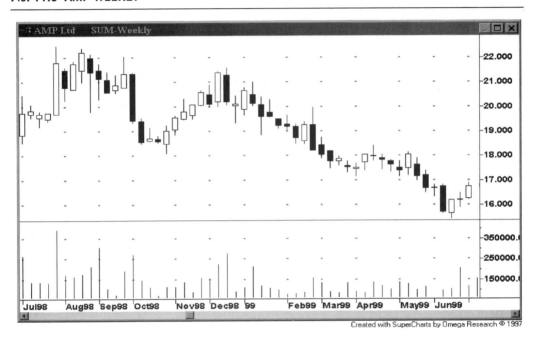

FIG. 11.7 AMP DAILY

➲ Analyse the share by drawing in trendlines, support and resistance lines, and observing the moving averages. Is your view bullish, bearish or is the share trending sideways?

➲ Do you want to write calls, puts or perform a strangle strategy for an end-of-the-month expiry?

➲ Where will you position your strike price?

➲ Review the options section in the newspaper clippings provided. Record the correct terminology to open your position.

2) *Time has passed and you are in week two of July. Review the share chart, (see Fig. 11.8). Have a look at the current options section of the newspaper in Table 11.6 and note the premiums available now on your written option positions. (If your chosen strike price is not included in this options table, it is likely that the premium has now been reduced to a negligible level, e.g. one cent. If this is the case, you have done very well!)*

Table 11.6 OPTIONS TABLE WEEK TWO

| CALL OPTIONS | | | | | | Friday 16 July 1999 |

Stock	Strike Price	Buyer	Seller	Last Sale	T.O. 000	Open Int.
AMP Last Sale Price $16.90						
1999						
Jul	16.00	.92	1.02	.90		411
Jul	16.50	.51	.58	.63	11	382
Jul	17.00	.23	.29	.26	8	1163
Jul	17.50	.07	.11	.12		1211

| PUT OPTIONS | | | | | | Friday 16 July 1999 |

Stock	Strike Price	Buyer	Seller	Last Sale	T.O. 000	Open Int.
AMP Last Sale Price $16.90						
1999						
Jul	16.00	.04	.07	.06		251
Jul	16.50	.10	.16	.26		504
Jul	17.00	.30	.36	.29	8	402
Jul	17.50	.64	.72	.67		161
Jul	18.00	1.04	1.18	2.44		20

FIG. 11.8 AMP DAILY

Created with SuperCharts by Omega Research ® 1997

➲ Has the premium gone down or up in response to the share price change?

↪ Based on the share price and option premiums in week two, determine whether you will take any defensive actions. If you are going to perform a defensive action, will you roll up, down, or simply close out? If you need to perform a defensive action, record the correct terminology and your existing profit/loss position for this transaction.

3) *You are now in week three of the month and only one week remains before your written option position expires. This will be your last opportunity to take defensive action prior to expiry. Take a look at the options table, (see Table 11.7), and the current share chart, (see Fig. 11.9).*

Table 11.7 OPTIONS TABLE WEEK THREE

CALL OPTIONS   **Friday 23 July 1999**

Stock	Strike Price	Buyer	Seller	Last Sale	T.O. 000	Open Int.
AMP Last Sale Price $17.08 1999						
Jul	16.00	1.03	1.17	1.09		411
Jul	16.50	.56	.68	.77		390
Jul	17.00			.25	40	1128
Jul	17.50	.05		.09	20	1141

PUT OPTIONS   **Friday 23 July 1999**

Stock	Strike Price	Buyer	Seller	Last Sale	T.O. 000	Open Int.
AMP Last Sale Price $17.08 1999						
Jul	16.50		.05	.04		380
Jul	17.00			.18	15	454

FIG. 11.9 AMP DAILY

Created with SuperCharts by Omega Research ® 1997

➲ Has the premium gone down or up in response to the share price change? If you are going to perform a defensive action, will you roll up, down, or simply close out? If you need to perform a defensive action, record the correct terminology and your existing profit/loss position for this transaction.

_____

_____

_____

_____

4) *It is now the day after the expiry day. Have a look at the share price activity on the chart, (see Fig. 11.10) and the option section from newspaper with data taken from the day of expiry, (Table 11.8). How did you go? Was your written position out-of-the-money on the expiry day? If it was, you did very well! You can keep the premium that you received when you first wrote the option. (I'm not sure what happened to the courier that I sent around to your house with the bag of money from Round 1... he must be lost! Sorry about that!)*

If you chose to write a $17.50 call, you would have received a premium of approximately 25¢. The closing price of AMP was $17.55 on the expiry day, so you would have ended up with an option that was 5¢ in-the-money. In reality, on the expiry day, it is likely that you would have closed out your position for approximately 7¢. The market makers who actually place your order will never just charge you the intrinsic value (5¢) as they are likely to mark up the price of the option by a few cents and pocket the difference. If this was the case, you would have made a profit of 18¢ (i.e. 25¢ minus 7¢).

NB. It is possible for unexpected fundamental issues to have an effect on the share price. In fact, a few days prior to expiry there was a significant change in the management structure at AMP. This is something that traders cannot predict.

Table 11.8 OPTIONS TABLE EXPIRY DAY

CALL OPTIONS   Friday 30 July 1999

Stock	Strike Price	Buyer	Seller	Last Sale	T.O. 000	Open Int.
AMP Last Sale Price $17.55 1999						
Jul	16.00	1.48	1.64	1.09		377
Jul	16.50	.99	1.13	1.10	4	408
Jul	17.00	.50	.62	.56	526	1303
Jul	17.50	.03	.09	.08	1053	1121

PUT OPTIONS   Friday 30 July 1999

Stock	Strike Price	Buyer	Seller	Last Sale	T.O. 000	Open Int.
AMP Last Sale Price $17.55 1999						
Jul	17.50		.01	.07	6	218
Jul	18.00	.38	.50	1.09	2	8

Fɪɢ. *11.10 AMP DAILY*

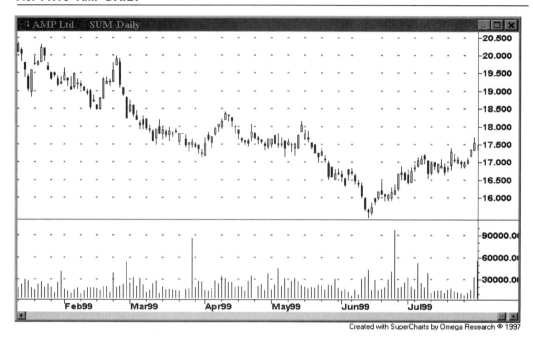

Created with SuperCharts by Omega Research ® 1997

⮑   If your option was in-the-money on the expiry day, it is likely
    that you will have been exercised. Were you happy for this to
    happen? Should you have taken a defensive action earlier in the
    month? Did you make a loss? What did you learn from this
    exercise?

    _____

    _____

    _____

    _____

Congratulations! You have just completed two paper trades. Even if you did
not come out with a profitable trade, you have no doubt added to your
knowledge about how to trade options. You are a hop, skip and a jump
away from making real money through writing options. If you are unhappy
with your results from this game, try it again choosing a different strike
price. With a bit of practice, you will be able to consistently make good
returns using this method.

➔   ➔   ➔   *Now that you have had a chance to practise your skills, it is time to have a look at*
        the paperwork that you need to monitor in order to trade effectively... ➔   ➔   ➔

Chapter Twelve

A PAPERWORK JUNGLE

It is essential to be aware of the administrative issues involved in trading options. One of the traders that I trained was a charismatic, but disorganised character. His option contracts were sometimes neatly placed in folders, and at other times they were thrown out, on a totally random basis. This was partially because this trader allowed his broker to open and close option positions without his full consultation and understanding. This led to a diminished sense of responsibility for the trader, and ultimately, disorganisation was the result. When I finally met this trader, he was extremely stressed and he had no idea which positions were open and which positions were threatened. This is obviously a very dangerous way to trade!

As traders, we must take responsibility for our own actions. Brokers will never care as much about our money as we will. Certainly, it would be far more effective for us to maintain control of our own trading and to carefully record our transactions, as well as our profit and loss.

A simple and easy-to-follow system is required that addresses the following issues:

➲ What are your open positions including your strike prices and premiums received?

➲ What have you earned in this month and this financial year?

➲ What defensive actions have you implemented?

➲ What is your exposure on both written puts and calls?

One of the simplest ways to keep track of your option trades is to use a spreadsheet. With a few formulae, it is possible to set up a sheet to tally your profit on a month-to-month basis as well as for the year. This will provide your accountant with a foundation for calculating your tax position. If you are using a portfolio manager as a part of your charting package, you could consider entering your share trades into the software that you own, but keeping your option transactions separately. This will give you the features that you desire from a portfolio manager, as well as the flexibility to keep your option trades in a format that is most suitable for your requirements. If you would like a copy of the Excel spreadsheet that I use, feel free to email me and I can provide it for you (there will be a fee for this). My contact details are listed at the back of this book.

It is important to cross-reference all your official options paperwork to the spreadsheet in order to ensure that all positions have been filled correctly, and that your stockbroker has accurately calculated your premiums and brokerage. I would suggest that you keep all option contracts and paperwork in separate folders for each month. This will assist in future cross-referencing should it be required.

Occasionally your stockbroker may make an error and either book someone else's option trade to your account, or provide you with a contract for the wrong strike price or expiry date. Without an effective administration system, it is likely that you will not realise that an error has been made. If you accept the paperwork and do not question your broker, you are technically accepting responsibility for the trade. If the trade turns sour, you may be liable for the loss incurred if you have not raised this issue with your broker, even though it was another trader who initially placed the order.

Full service brokers are terrific for sorting out little messes such as this. If you are dealing with an Internet brokerage firm, it may be difficult to resolve any issues that you may have with incorrectly processed orders. Rene Rivken, one of Australia's best known traders, commented at a World Masters of Business Conference (30 May 1999): "Giving people the power to use Internet broking is like giving people the power to poison themselves".

In my opinion it makes better business sense to trade with an experienced options broker, rather than rely on the Internet for options trading. This is especially true when you are learning about the options market. An experienced broker will provide you with value far beyond the cost of the brokerage fees.

Here are some suggested headings that you could use to construct an appropriate spreadsheet:

Bank Account Information

Fees

Interest

Margin Loan Data

Exposure

Level of Put Option Exposure

Level of Call Option Exposure

Total Profit/Loss

For each month

For the year

Written Positions

Open Positions

Defensive Actions

Exercised Positions

Fees

OCH fees

Brokerage

WHAT TYPE OF PAPERWORK CAN YOU EXPECT?

You will receive several types of paperwork when you begin trading options. Some brokerage firms produce their own records to send out to clients rather than relying on the paperwork generated from the OCH. This situation is becoming increasingly common. Although differences in paperwork may be apparent between brokerage firms, in general, you can expect to receive records that reflect the following information:

- Bank Account Statements
- Contract Note/Liquidation Advice Statements
- Statement of Accounts
- Open Position Statements
- Margin Loan Statements (if you have set up a margin loan)
- Buy and Sell Contracts for shares (if you are buying and selling shares).

BANK ACCOUNT STATEMENTS

Bank account statements detail the debits and credits relating to your account. Usually you are required to set up a cash management account linked to your Options Clearing House account. For every option position that you write, the OCH or your brokerage firm reserves some cash or shares as security. This is often referred to as a 'margin'. Be aware that this definition differs entirely from your 'margin loan'.

Liaise with your broker to find out exactly how he or she works and ensure that all broker documentation is signed before placing your first order. Ensure that sufficient funds are available for margin and security purposes and that your cash management account is suitable for the purpose of writing options.

For written options, the OCH or your brokerage firm calculates a daily margin based on the movement of the share in relation to the strike price for all written positions. This margin is re-calculated to compensate for changes in the market conditions and the calculated amount is held by the OCH in a separate account. The OCH will usually provide interest on any cash margin that it retains. This is comparable to the current rate on a cash management account. If you trade aggressively, the margins required by the OCH will be greater than if you write more conservative option positions.

The OCH can also hold some, or all, of your shares as 'margin' if they are included on its list of approved shares. You can stipulate whether you would like the OCH to control cash or shares. The OCH will value the share portfolio at less-than-the-market value in order to accommodate any fall in value that your portfolio may experience.

It is wise to always consider margin requirements. If you do not have adequate funds or shares to cover the requirements, you will be 'margin called'. In other words, you will be expected to come up with the required margin within a limited time frame, otherwise it is possible that the OCH will sell shares that you own or liquidate some of your positions. Consult with your broker to find out how much margin the OCH will require, and if in doubt, do not open any new positions until you are certain that these requirements have been fulfilled.

CONTRACT NOTE/LIQUIDATION ADVICE STATEMENTS

Whenever you open or close a transaction, you are sent a Contract Note/ Liquidation Advice. (Some brokerage firms have different names for the various pieces of paperwork that they send.) This records the position that you opened or closed, the expiry date, the number of contracts and details of any brokerage/fees.

It is essential that you read this statement carefully to ensure that all details have been accurately recorded. If there is an error, ring your broker and query the error immediately. By accepting the paperwork for a contract that you did not write, you are implying that you are accepting this position. If you do not bring this to your broker's immediate attention, it is possible that by implication, you are accepting any losses that are incurred through this position. Some brokerage firms impose time limits for this type of query, so do not accept any erroneous paperwork!

STATEMENT OF ACCOUNT

This statement details all debits and credits into and out of your OCH account. By looking at this statement, you can obtain a clear idea of any margin amount retained by the OCH. Each transaction you have made throughout the month is listed for you. Some brokerage firms list the statement of account on the same sheet as the open position statement and the contract note/liquidation advice.

OPEN POSITION STATEMENTS

Open position statements detail all of the written positions that are booked to your account and give you a summary of those due to expire. Some brokerage firms send out paperwork listing your open positions on a daily basis. Other firms provide these on a monthly basis.

MARGIN LOAN STATEMENTS

A margin loan operates for the express purpose of buying shares using loaned money. It can usually be established in conjunction with your brokerage firm by providing some form of security such as cash or shares. Although many traders utilise margin lending, if you are a beginner in the sharemarket you need to be aware of the risks involved. Margin lending is usually used by very experienced traders only.

If you are determined to establish a margin loan, you need to consider whether to provide cash as collateral, or to provide shares. Keep in mind that your shares will be valued at less than the actual market value. Usually the valuation of your shares will be at 70% of their total market value. Not all shares can be utilised as collateral for a margin loan. The approved shares are usually of the blue chip variety and your brokerage firm will be able to provide you with guidelines on this issue.

Some brokerage firms will allow you to set up a margin loan in advance, and hold this service open to you should you need to utilise it. This has many important implications for option writers. In terms of exposure, it is essential that you can cover the contracts that you have written, particularly with written puts. By establishing a margin loan and placing this loan 'on hold', you can approximately double the exposure level that you can handle. For example, instead of writing puts to the level of $100,000 exposure, you can use your margin loan to expose yourself to the value of $200,000.

SHARE CONTRACTS

If you have been trading already, you will be familiar with the buy and sell contracts that you receive when performing share transactions. If you are exercised on any written contracts, you will receive notification from your broker. This will include an appropriate contract note/liquidation advice to show that you have been exercised, as well as the usual buy and sell contracts for the shares that were covered by the option contract. It is highly likely that these contract notes will be converted to an electronic format in the future.

Check the capital gains/income tax implications of the income that you derive through trading options with your accountant. If you are audited you will require copies of the original paperwork. Careful record-keeping will alleviate any pressures that you may feel if you are subjected to an audit.

Now the paperwork is under control, let us move onto the essential area of gaining control over our minds.

Trading Secrets

Carefully cross-reference each piece of paperwork to your records and query any missing or erroneous transactions immediately.

➔ ➔ ➔ *Have you ever wondered why the percentage of losers in the sharemarket has stayed consistent for the last 100 years, despite the fact that there is more information today than ever before about trading?*
Keep reading to find out how to use your mind to make money... ➔ ➔ ➔

Chapter Thirteen

THE EMOTIONAL ROLLERCOASTER

WHY DO PEOPLE STOP OPTIONS TRADING?

There are a lot of horror stories about people's experiences trading options. Some of these stories may be based on truth, so it is important to know why people are sometimes repelled from trading options after being introduced to the market.

By ignoring your own risk tolerance and letting discipline in your option trading habits slide, the day will come when you will make an error in trading which will cost you dearly. When you are in a trade where you have ignored your own risk tolerance level, you will be subject to stress and emotional turmoil. This, in turn, leads to making poor trading decisions such as not taking defensive action when it is necessary. A loss under these conditions typically leads traders to lose confidence in their own abilities and some people in this situation decide never to trade again! However, by following my system of trading options, along with developing your own emotional mastery, it is unlikely that you will become one of these tortured traders who suffer dire consequences.

HANDLING THE WINS

Ego is an amazing thing, isn't it? Just enough egoism is necessary to give us the courage to trade, but if you become arrogant then you will make poor trading decisions based on the belief that you could not possibly be wrong. Greed takes over. Before you know it, you are facing a loss that you do not want to realise because you were so sure your analysis was correct.

When I first started trading I oscillated between joy and despair, joy and despair, joy and despair … and that was all within the first five minutes of entering a trade! Over time I have learned to gain some control over my emotions, but it is still a challenge that all traders must face.

In his book called *Let The Trade Wins Flow*, Dr Harry E. Stanton states that:

> *"Successful traders are continually striving to be the best traders they can be, [and] this is of more importance than making money. When this is so, the problem of emotional indiscipline is virtually overcome for when the all-embracing focus is upon trading well, rather than on making money, the power of greed and fear is vastly reduced."*

As I have a degree in psychology, the mind of the trader began to fascinate me, (especially since I was experiencing many of these psychological effects first-hand). Once I became aware of my reactions, I had more of a chance of mastering my emotions. Knowledge is the key.

Table 13.1 WHY DO PEOPLE STOP OPTIONS TRADING?

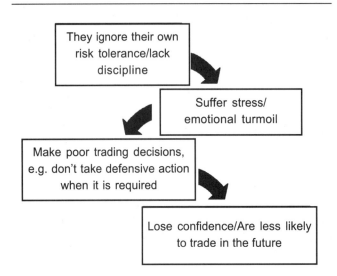

They ignore their own risk tolerance/lack discipline

Suffer stress/ emotional turmoil

Make poor trading decisions, e.g. don't take defensive action when it is required

Lose confidence/Are less likely to trade in the future

When you have made a loss, how do you react? There is nothing more debilitating than the emotional reaction that many traders experience after taking a loss. You may feel drained of energy, or perhaps you would like revenge on the market and as a result, enter foolish trading positions. If you can understand your likely reactions, you will be more inclined to overcome your own emotional responses.

One of the main concepts that affects traders is the principle of cognitive dissonance.

COGNITIVE DISSONANCE

Cognitive dissonance is the tendency to reject information that is contrary to the trading decision that has just been made, and to look for information to confirm that the trader is correct.

No-one likes to be wrong, so people will often look for evidence that they are right, rather than accept the fact that they are not perfect.

Imagine that you have just purchased a new BMW. What a wonderful feeling you experience as you zoom around to your neighbours and relatives showing off your new acquisition. When you drive up to your brother-in-law's house, he rushes out to inform you that BMWs have just rated below Volvo in terms of Australia's most desired car. You now have a choice... either you can believe your brother-in-law and feel miserable, or you can reject everything he has said and decide to feel good about your BMW purchase. To confirm your view you may read about BMW's magnificent safety record, superb design and superior resale value.

So often people seek out confirming information and reject contrary information. This can be very damaging to a trader's bank balance. If a trader is in a trade and that share has made money, he is bound to feel nice warm emotions of gratitude to that share for supplying a profit. That share could become a 'favourite'.

BHP became the favourite share for many Australians. A lot of traders made thousands of dollars on the back of the bullish wave that BHP rode for many years. What happened when BHP started moving sideways and then dropping dramatically in value? (BHP slid from a high of over $20.00 in 1997 to a low of under $11.00 in early 1999.)

Objectively, it would have made sense to jump out of this trade at some stage in 1998. However, if you are subject to cognitive dissonance, you are likely to search the papers to find stories about how wonderful BHP is. You will revel in broker reports that the share price could increase by 40% in three months, and that its expansion plans are well underway.

By ignoring the facts, and hoping that BHP will go up, despite the information displayed on the share chart, you lose your objectivity. Unfortunately, it is impossible to control a share's price action by the sheer power of your will. As soon as you find yourself willing a share in a particular direction, it is unlikely that your objectivity is at its highest level.

You may be a victim of cognitive dissonance if you:

➲ Focus on good news about the share, even though you are losing capital.

➲ Tend to buy more of a downtrending stock to prove you are right.

➲ 'Shut yourself off' from everything to do with trading, only to suffer horrible losses due to neglecting your portfolio.

➲ Start hoping that a stock will go down so your written calls will be safe.

➲ Start hoping that a stock will go up so your written puts will be safe.

RESPONSE ABILITY

As a trader, you learn more quickly from your mistakes if you are willing to take responsibility for your actions. If you break down the word 'responsibility', you can see that it consists of two components; 'response' and 'ability'. To a large degree, your success as a trader will be determined by your *ability* to detect changes in market trends and *respond* in an appropriate manner to these changes.

We all know people who are continually blaming outside influences for their own misfortunes. They blame their mother, their neighbour, the weather, their education level, the colour of their hair, etc., in order to provide an excuse for their own lack of performance. This feeling of 'it wasn't my fault' causes many learning opportunities to be missed.

When traders lose money, they usually blame bad luck, poor advice, etc., rather than their own personal attributes of arrogance, fear and greed. Locus of control is an important determinant of success. An internal locus of control is the tendency to take responsibility for all situations. An external locus of control is the tendency to believe that outside forces control everything.

Traders with an internal locus of control:

➲ Have a high level of self-belief.

➲ Know that they are completely responsible for their own actions.

➲ Do not rely predominantly on 'expert advice', e.g. brokers' opinions, newspapers.

➲ Know that they cannot control the markets, only themselves.

➲ React objectively.

Traders with an external locus of control:

⮕ Experience frequent self-doubt.

⮕ Blame their broker or 'experts' when they make a loss.

⮕ Have trouble learning from past experience because they do not take responsibility.

⮕ Try to prove that they are right rather than minimising their losses when a trade turns against them.

⮕ React emotionally.

QUALITIES OF THE EXPERT TRADER

Expert traders take responsibility and react objectively at all times. It is almost as if they do not have their own money invested in the market. They have developed a sense of detachment from their profit and loss results and instead, aim only to trade well. They do not rely on the advice of others and tend to make their own decisions based on sound analysis. They definitely maintain an internal locus of control. Here are some of these qualities in more detail:

⮕ Wins and losses are indistinguishable in terms of their emotional state.

⮕ If the market does not 'behave', expert traders take unemotional action to limit risk.

⮕ They analyse their winning and losing trades and learn from their experience.

⮕ They have a written list of back-tested trading rules and follow them without exception.

⮕ They trade to follow their rules and to trade well, rather than chase profits.

How can these coveted skills be developed?

TRADING DIARY

My key to developing objectivity is to keep a trading diary. I record all of my thoughts and analysis prior to entering a trade in a two-ring A4 binder. I calculate my projections based on technical analysis of a share chart and I analyse whether my arguments for entering the trade will stand up when I write them down. If I cannot justify my trade on paper, I will not perform the trade using my own money. My diary is my secret tool to developing objectivity. I have a chance to present the views of a total optimist, and then to play devil's advocate.

When I have made a loss, my diary provides insight into my mindset prior to entering the trade. After making a profit *or* a loss I ask:

➲ What did I do well?

➲ What would I do differently if I were to repeat this trade?

I record the answers to these two questions regardless of the result of my trade. Both winning and losing trades teach you certain lessons. Losing trades often provide the greatest opportunities for personal growth as traders. I still consider that one of my best trades (where I followed my rules to the letter) was a situation that eventuated in my taking a loss. Regardless of the profit/loss situation, a *good trade* is made when you stay true to your trading rules.

The simple practice of maintaining a trading diary has helped me to detect incorrect assumptions, bad habits and poor trading techniques. Your skills of the future lie in your ability to analyse your weaknesses and strengths of the past.

Trading Secrets

Your level of financial success rarely exceeds your level of self-development.

➔ ➔ ➔ *Now that you are thinking like a winner, why don't you have a look at how you can get yourself set up to trade effectively by developing a trading plan? Keep reading to find out how...* ➔ ➔ ➔

Chapter Fourteen

READY, SET,... GO

In trading years ahead you will meet many people, if you haven't met them already, who fancy themselves as sharemarket experts and will take great pleasure in telling you what you should be doing in the market. The sad truth is that these individuals are full of advice but often never actually *do* anything themselves. You would be surprised how many self-proclaimed experts fall into this category. Usually they have not set for themselves a goal, any rules, or even a business/trading plan.

To get a business off the ground, it is essential to have a business plan. This provides guidance for future activities and assists in setting clear strategic objectives.

If you are serious about trading as a part-time or full-time career, it is essential that you make the effort to design a clear trading plan. I suggest that you develop a set of rules that you can use to guide your trading, and check your plan periodically. Write down your plan on paper and once you have a list of effective rules, follow the rules rather than strive to make a profit. Money will be made as a by-product of following your rules. By merely chasing profits, you often become subject to the emotion of greed that will diminish your effectiveness as a trader.

A trading plan for writing options should include the following:

➲ When to enter a trade.

➲ When to exit a trade.

➲ What is the minimum premium you are prepared to accept on a monthly basis?

➲ What is the amount of capital available that you are prepared to commit to the options market?

➲ What is the amount of capital that you are willing to risk on any given trade?

➲ When you make a profit or a loss, how are you going to manage your money?

You will have to think long and hard about many of these questions. Traders who do not make these decisions in advance may profit in the short term. One day, however, they will come unstuck when a trade turns against them.

After you have made a win or two, there is a tendency to continue increasing your exposure or number of contracts. Traders in this situation often tend to write closer to the money options and forget any rules regarding exposure. They become overconfident and believe that they have the skills to *conquer* the market! Their overconfidence leads them to take greater and greater risks with larger numbers of contracts. This is an incredibly dangerous situation.

Decide in advance the level of risk that you are willing to accept, and develop a contingency plan in case the trade turns against your initial view. Remember to back-test your system in order to see its effectiveness using actual trading examples.

When developing your rules, remember the SMART principle. By setting SMART goals and objectives you are giving yourself a fighting chance of performing to your maximum potential. Your objectives should be:

➲ **S**pecific

➲ **M**easurable

➲ **A**chievable

➲ **R**ealistic

➲ **T**o a Time Frame.

QUICK REFERENCE GUIDE

I feel that is important for you to develop a list of your own trading rules. This will mean more to you than following someone else's rules verbatim. However, throughout each chapter, I have given you snippets of my rules. Here is a quick reference guide to summarise the shorter-term option writing secrets that I follow each month.

- ⮑   I trade at the end of week one or the start of week two for an end-of-month expiry for naked calls. For covered calls, I trade at the end of week one for an expiry within one to three months.

- ⮑   I trade the following shares when writing options: BHP (BHP), CWO (Optus), NCP (News Corp), AMP (AMP), WPL (Woodside), TLS (Telstra), RIO (Rio Tinto), LLC (Lend Lease), ANZ (ANZ Bank), WBC (Westpac Bank), CBA (Commonwealth Bank) and NAB (National Australia Bank). At the time of writing, these shares have sufficient volume and offer the best premiums. I review this list at least once a year to ensure that I am involved in liquid option positions.

- ⮑   I write calls for downtrending/lateral shares, or beyond the price that I believe the share will reach if the upward movement appears to be running out of momentum.

- ⮑   I write puts for uptrending/lateral shares, or beyond the price that I believe the share will reach if the downward movement appears to be running out of momentum.

- ⮑   I decide how many contracts to write based on the level of exposure that I can cover financially.

- ⮑   When writing puts and calls I choose a strike price a minimum of one resistance/support level away from the current price or beyond the price that I feel the share will reach. If I can obtain two resistance/support levels away from the current price and still get a reasonable premium, this is preferable.

- ⮑   I refuse to trade unless I can get a *minimum* 5¢ premium per share per month, for the initial transaction. I am not willing to accept the 'risk' of trading for less than this amount.

- ⮑   When rolling up or down or out, I only roll once — EVER! I only roll up or down if I can achieve a strike price that is a minimum of one significant resistance level away. I only roll out if I am writing covered calls.

➲ For naked calls and uncovered puts, if there is a strong day that penetrates the strike price by greater than the premium initially received within week one, two or three of the month, then I automatically close out the next day. If I am in week four, and the strike price is penetrated or threatened, I use my own judgement whether or not to close out. I may wait until the expiry day and close out in the final hour if necessary (in order to minimise time value still apparent in the price of the premium).

➲ I look for opportunities to close out puts from an early stage in the month. I close out on puts more aggressively than on calls because puts are more likely to be exercised prior to expiry.

➲ At all times, these rules take precedence over any analytical chart observation.

Some people are more skilled at short-term trading while others prefer medium-term positions or long-term positions. You will develop your own personal style and this will determine whether you are more comfortable with short expiry dates, or longer-term expiry dates.

This list of rules is not an iron-clad guarantee to making money in the options market. The skills that you acquire in analysing the direction of the share is equally important as determining the ideal options strategy for you. This is a fact that is often neglected by budding option traders.

If you are new to the sharemarket, I suggest that you begin with a medium-term view. Try trading shares before you try your hand at the options market. Spend six months at least learning about technical analysis and share trading. You can treat this time as an apprenticeship. This apprenticeship provides a vital foundation. By beginning with share trading, you will develop many of the skills required to trade options successfully. Many people try to skip this valuable step of skill development through medium-term trend analysis. In doing so they deny themselves important learning opportunities.

Trading Secrets

▸ *Develop a trading plan to guide your trading activities.*

▸ *Begin with a medium-term view in trading shares prior to delving into the options market.*

SEVEN GOLDEN OPTION WRITING RULES

Below are the seven most important rules to observe when trading options:

1) Trade with the trend

Standing in the path of an oncoming avalanche is a potential accident waiting to happen. It would be far safer to stay behind the avalanche and watch it tumble away from you! For this reason, if you write puts under a downtrending share, you'd better be completely sure that the downward thrust has run out of steam and that an upturn is likely. Writing a call in this situation may be a much wiser decision.

If a share has been uptrending strongly, writing a call may provide unacceptable levels of risk if the trend does not reverse! It is wiser to write a call if the share is trending down, and write a put if the share is trending up. This is especially true when you are starting out in the options market. If the share is trending sideways, you could write both puts and calls.

2) Don't Let Pride Get in Your Way

If the share chart is telling you a story that you refuse to believe, you could be a victim of the devastating effects of 'pride'. If you remain flexible and responsive to the charts, it is possible to completely alter the direction of your view. If you've written a put option, and the share trends down, you can always close out this position and then write a call... but only if you are prepared to swallow your pride. Often in trading, the enemy is not the market, nor your broker. The enemy is your own mindset.

3) Know Your Acceptable Risk Level

There is no shame in being a conservative player in the market. If you are not comfortable with higher levels of risk, do not place aggressive orders.

Make sure that your analysis is extremely good and that you are placing yourself in a trade that has a high probability of success based on the indicators. The simplest way to increase the returns you receive in trading options is to write closer-to-the-money or in-the-money options. Instead of writing an option two resistance/support levels away from the price, you could experiment with writing at a strike price one resistance/support level away.

Your level of aggression will be rewarded if the trade goes your way, but if it does not, you must be prepared to live with the consequences. The consequences in options equate to higher levels of loss per trade. Personally, I only write out-of-the-money options.

4)   Know Your Term

Know the term of your trade before you take a position. There is a saying that I have heard brokers quote: "There's another day trader turned long-term investor". The practice of rolling out to a later month often encourages sloppy trading habits. If your view is not fulfilled in the set time frame that you have estimated, it shows a lack of discipline to extend the time frame.

You must know how long you are prepared to be in the trade, prior to placing your order. Writing shorter-term options will lessen your chances of the trade turning against you, but it will provide lower premiums. Writing longer-term options will maximise your premiums, but your risk factor also increases accordingly.

5)   Never Deal in Illiquid Options

If a trade turns against you in a liquid position, you can usually buy back your options at will. This is not the case if you deal in illiquid options. If you want to close out as a defensive action, there may be no willing market for you to do so. This is a terrifying situation.

There is a trader I know who happens to be a Vietnam War veteran. He once referred to the fear that he felt when he was trapped in a losing trade to being the same level of fear that he faced when fighting on the front line! (I am sure that his reference to this was somewhat tongue in cheek.)

Save yourself from unnecessary stress by refusing to deal in illiquid options.

6)   Close out Written Puts Earlier than Written Calls

As the preceding chapters revealed, written puts are more at risk in market corrections or in significant retracements. In addition, they are more likely to be exercised early because of the personal stake on the part of buyers to free up their capital. For this reason, it pays to be particularly responsive in relation to your written puts. If they are threatened, close out! In the case of your written calls, closing out at an early stage is not quite as urgent.

7)   Never Let Your Losses Run

If you lack discipline in being able to take a loss, you may have difficulty trading in the options market. Trading options is not for everybody. Recognise your own strengths and weaknesses and be prepared to maximise your strengths. If you struggle with discipline, perhaps stay with shares.

How To Get Started Trading Options

Common mistakes that beginners to the option market make include ignoring their own risk tolerance levels, overtrading and performing complex spreads before they are ready. To avoid these errors, I have suggested the following steps to start you off gradually. By plunging into complex, aggressive positions prematurely, traders risk disappointment and loss.

1) *Consult with your broker to assess if any specific paperwork needs to be completed prior to trading.* Inform your broker of your plan to trade options and ensure that he has a clear understanding of the options market and the strategy that you are about to implement. If your broker lacks experience in this area, I suggest that you find another broker.

2) *Try at least a few trades on paper at first.* If you have not completed *The Options Game* in Chapter 11, do this now! This will assist in giving you a chance to understand how options work before risking your capital. However, no matter how clever you are at paper-trading, there is nothing like putting your own money into the market and experiencing the ultimate emotional rollercoaster. The effect of your emotions has a very real impact on your ability as a trader.

3) *Prior to opening your first options position, form a clear view on the direction of the trend of a share.* Once you have formed a view and chosen your strike price, review the option premiums detailed in your newspaper. This will help you to narrow down your option selections based on the premiums available.

4) *Begin by writing an out-of-the-money call on a downtrending stock, or over a share that you already own.* I would suggest that you start on a small scale and then work your way up in terms of exposure and the complexity of your trading positions. If you write one contract, this will cover 1000 shares in total. You will probably make an overall loss when you take into account transaction costs, but you will be gaining valuable experience. By watching the prices of your written position, you will begin to see an actual example of how the share price affects your option premiums.

5) *Place your orders with your broker and make sure that you have confirmation verbally as well as receiving the appropriate paperwork to show that your orders have been filled.* Remember to record all details in order to keep track of all open positions. Check on the paperwork carefully and cross-reference this to your spreadsheet. Monitor your trades on a daily basis as a minimum. If any of your positions are being threatened, it is wise to monitor at least twice during the day, as well as at the end of the day.

6) *Each day make a decision whether to close out or hold open your position.* It is suggested that you do not implement other defensive actions such as rolling down or up, until you have gained a deeper

understanding of the options market. Closing out should be your only defensive action.

7) *On the expiry day, you will need to close out any in-the-money options if you do not wish to be exercised.* If you want to be an active options trader, you must be prepared to set aside at least 30 to 60 minutes a day to monitor your positions and review your view on the direction of a share's trend. Be especially vigilant on the expiry day.

Once you have made a few conservative trades, within three months or so, you will have developed vital skills and knowledge. This will give you the confidence required to try some slightly more aggressive trades if you desire. Give yourself a pat on the back for approaching the market conservatively. By continuing to cultivate skill in analysis and knowledge about options, you will substantially add to your cashflow as well as your return on investment.

Another excellent reference to assist you in this field is *Understanding Options Trading in Australia* by Chris Tate. I know that you will benefit from Chris's knowledge of this topic.

You have now begun to discover the secrets of professional option writers and have valuable techniques available that can lead to greater financial returns. As a fellow trader, I would like to welcome you to the field of option writing and wish you all the best in your future trading endeavours.

Happy Trading!

GLOSSARY

AT-MARKET OR AT-THE-MARKET: An order to buy or sell an option or share at the prevailing market price.

AT-THE-MONEY: When the exercise price of the option is close to or equal to the current market price.

AVERAGE DOWN: Buying more of a security that is declining in price (after originally buying it at a higher price) to lower the average price paid for it — not recommended.

BACK-TEST: A method of testing an indicator's performance by applying it to historical data.

BEAR/BEARISH: A trader with a negative expectation of the market or a particular share. Some texts use this phrase to signify a sideways trending market as well as a downtrending market. For the sake of simplicity, this book refers to 'bearish' as representing a downtrending market or share.

BULL/BULLISH: A trader with a positive expectation that prices will rise in the market or for a particular share.

BUYING OPTIONS: See _writing options._

BUY AND WRITE STRATEGY: See _covered calls._

CANDLESTICKS: A 17th century Japanese technique that uses the same information that is contained in a western bar chart, but provides a different graphic representation. Candlestick patterns of 1, 2 or 3 candles (bars) provide an excellent timing/confirmation tool when used in conjunction with other indicators.

CALL OPTION: A call option gives the buyer the right, but not the obligation, to buy a given security at a particular price up to and including the day of expiry.

CLOSE-OFF: The day an option expires. See also *expiry date*.

COGNITIVE DISSONANCE: Cognitive dissonance is the tendency to reject information which is contrary to the trading decision that has just been made, and to look for information to confirm that the trader is correct (in order to alleviate any psychological discomfort the trader is experiencing). None of us likes to be 'wrong', so we often look for evidence that we are 'right', rather than accept the fact that we are fallible.

CONTRACT: Options are sold by the contract. One option contract usually covers 1000 shares. For example, five BHP options contracts would cover 5000 BHP shares.

CORRECTION: A movement in prices against the general trend which typically occurs with little or no warning. For instance, the market periodically loses value as many of the underlying securities drop in price by several per cent.

COVERED CALLS: In this situation the writer of the call option owns the underlying shares.

DEFENSIVE ACTIONS: These are used as a last resort when the share goes against the view you had when initially writing the option. Defensive actions are a way of removing yourself from risk and minimising your potential loss if the trade goes against you — strategies include rolling up, rolling down, closing out and rolling out.

DELTA: The sensitivity of an option price to a change in the underlying share price.

DERIVATIVES: A derivative is a financial instrument which is based on another product such as a share or index. Its leverage is greater than that of the product from which it is derived. Options and futures are the most commonly traded derivatives.

DIVIDEND: A periodic payment (usually twice a year) to shareholders from a company's net profit.

DOUBLE TOP: A pattern of price action which appears on chart displays as two price rallies in quick succession which stop at or near the same high. This often signifies that a downtrend is imminent.

DOW OR DOW JONES: The US-based share index.

DOWNTREND: Where prices make consistently lower highs and lower lows.

EX-DIVIDEND: This refers to the period spanning the announcement and payment of a dividend. Those who buy the shares after a share has gone ex-dividend will not receive the dividend. The share price tends to rise as the actual ex-dividend date approaches (when the dividend is paid), and there is typically a drop in the share price on the day after the dividend is paid.

EXERCISE: This is when option buyers choose to take up their right to buy or sell the shares covered by an option. They can do this at or before the expiry date. It is likely to occur, however, only after the share price has risen above the strike price of the option, or if there is a vested interest to exercise due to the effect of an ex-dividend scenario.

EXPIRY DATE: The final date of the option contract. The duration of each option contract will often be 12 months or more. As a writer, you can choose to write contracts on options at any time before expiry. The choice is up to you.

EXPONENTIAL MOVING AVERAGE (EMA): A moving average indicator which takes the sum of closing price data and averages them. It plots points which, when connected, form a line. This line smooths the fluctuations present when looking at price action on a chart. EMA analysis attaches more importance to the most recent data than the older data, on an exponential basis.

EXPOSURE: As a writer, this is the total possible amount of money that you would be liable for if the options were to be exercised.

FUNDAMENTALS: Fundamental analysis assists in detecting *which* shares have a probability of increasing or decreasing in value based on a company's accounts, for example its balance sheet and profit/loss details.

EXCHANGE-TRADED OPTIONS: The options traded over shares in Australia are called 'exchange-traded options' or 'American-style options'. This type of option allows the holder to exercise the option at any time during the life of the contract.

GAPS: Gaps show that the price activity of the preceding period is completely above or below the next candlestick or bar apparent on the chart.

HISTORIC VOLATILITY: The standard deviation of the share price changes over a particular time period which will match the time until expiry of your option.

ILLIQUID: Options with low levels of trading are considered 'illiquid' and are best avoided. If trading in illiquid options, and the trade goes against you, exiting from your open positions will be considerably more difficult than with frequently-traded options.

IMPLIED VOLATILITY: The market's current assessment of volatility based upon the current option's price.

IN-THE-MONEY: A call option with a strike price below the share price, or a put option with a strike price above the share price, is termed in-the-money.

LIQUID: Options with high levels of trading.

MACD (MOVING AVERAGE CONVERGENCE DIVERGENCE): An indicator that plots the difference between two moving averages, which can be used to generate buy and sell signals.

MARKET MAKERS: These are the intermediaries between the brokers and the market. They set the price of the option based on prevailing market conditions and the level of risk, etc.

MOMENTUM: The velocity of a price trend. Momentum indicators show whether prices are declining at a faster or slower pace.

MOVING AVERAGE: See *Exponential Moving Average*.

NAKED CALLS: In this situation the writer of the call does not own the underlying security.

OPEN INTEREST: The number of outstanding option contracts at a particular strike price. This is a comparable concept to liquidity/volume.

OPTIONS CLEARING HOUSE (OCH): The official body that registers all option trades and maintains an orderly options market.

OUT-OF-THE-MONEY: When the share price is below the strike price of a call option, or when the share price is above the strike price of a put option. A recommended method in this book is to write out-of-the-money call and put options.

PAPER TRADE: Not trading with real money. Such 'practice' transactions are recorded and monitored as if a real position had been taken.

PREMIUM: This is the price of the option. For example, you may receive a 30¢ premium when writing an option.

PULLBACK: A downward retracement.

PUT OPTION: A put option gives the buyer the right, but not the obligation, to sell a given security at a certain price within a given time.

RALLY: An upward movement in prices after downward or sideways movements.

REGISTERED TRADERS: See *market makers*.

RETRACEMENT: A less significant version of a *correction*.

RESISTANCE: A level at which prices stall — sellers want to exit the market and buyers are reluctant to make a new high.

SELLING OPTIONS: See *writing options*.

SIDEWAYS TREND: A period of lateral price movement within a relatively narrow price band.

SLIPPAGE: The difference in the share or option price from the time of placing the order to the time it is executed.

SUPPORT: A level through which the price does not drop — there is more demand from buyers than supply from sellers.

STRIKE PRICE: The price at which you can buy (when you have written a call option) or sell (when you have written a put option) the underlying security; also known as the exercise price.

TECHNICAL ANALYSIS: The examination of price and volume action on a chart, using technical indicators, to reach conclusions about the likely direction of future price activity.

UPTREND: Where prices make consistently higher highs and higher lows.

VOLATILITY: A measure of fluctuation in market prices. Choppy shares with greater distances from the peak to the trough of their prices are more volatile and options related to these shares will attract higher premiums. For shares with a lower volatility level, the option premiums will also be lower. Volatility in the options market usually refers to *Historic* or *Implied* volatility.

WRITING OPTIONS: Option writers collect a premium or fee from an option buyer and subsequently, they are obligated to fulfil the request of the option buyer. In relation to call options, writers must *sell* their shares, or have the shares 'called away' from them, if a buyer decides to exercise his or her right. Put option writers are under obligation to *buy* the shares from a put option taker should they be exercised. You may be exercised at any time throughout the duration of the option contract. See also *exercise*.

FURTHER READING

Bedford, Louise, *The Secret of Candlestick Charting*, Wrightbooks, 2000.

Bedford, Louise, *Trading Secrets*, Wrightbooks, 2001.

Nison, Steve, *Japanese Candlestick Charting Techniques*, USA, 1991.

Stanton, Dr Harry E., *Let the Trade Wins Flow*, Copyright Dr H.E. Stanton, 1997.

Tate, Christopher, *The Art of Trading 2nd Edition*, Wrightbooks, 2001.

Tate, Christopher, *Understanding Options Trading in Australia*, Wrightbooks, 1997.

Tate, Christopher, *The Art of Derivatives Trading in Australia*, Wrightbooks, Available July 2002.

Temby, Christopher, *Trading Stock Options and Warrants 3rd Edition*, Wrightbooks, 2001.

Weinstein, Stan, *Secrets for Profiting in Bull and Bear Markets*, Irwin Professional Publishing, 1988.

ACKNOWLEDGMENTS

I would like to thank some special people whose contributions made this book possible:

▸ My husband **Chris Bedford,** whose editing and illustrating skills are unsurpassed.

▸ **Chris Tate** and **Harry Stanton,** for their practical assistance, suggestions and advice. You have both been my mentors from afar for many years.

▸ My sister **Valerie Laver** for always believing in me.

▸ To many of my clients who have provided valuable support and encouragement, including **Sue Chapman**, **Jim Edwards** and **Melinda Ash**.

▸ My futures broker, **Paul Ash** at **Peter G Moloney & Associates:**
Level 5, 45 William Street, Melbourne, Vic., 3000
Telephone: (03) 9629 4233 or **1800 621 927.**

▸ **Gary Stone** and the team at **ShareFinder Investment Services** for providing the opportunity for me to present strategies to their clients.
PO Box 349, Black Rock, Vic., 3193
Telephone: (03) 9589 0300.

INDEX

www.tradingsecrets.com.au

Consultancy Services

Trading Secrets Pty Ltd holds seminars and training sessions on a regular basis. Individual coaching is available for share and option traders wishing to substantially add to their profits and maximise their cashflow. Topics for seminars and coaching sessions include:

- ➤ The Secret of Writing Options
- ➤ Charting the Sharemarket
- ➤ The Secret of Candlestick Charting
- ➤ The Psychology of Trading
- ➤ Using Charting Software
- ➤ Candlestick Charting Home Study Course

- ➤ Option Buying Strategies
- ➤ Creating a Share Trading System
- ➤ How to Handle Volatile Markets
- ➤ Bear Market Trading
- ➤ Options Administration (including spreadsheet software)

For more information regarding these services, visit:

www.tradingsecrets.com.au

Trading Secrets Pty Ltd
PO Box 4094
Balwyn 3103